FOR STANDARDS
IN EDUCATION

Handbook for Inspecting
SPECIAL SCHOOLS
AND PUPIL REFERRAL UNITS
with guidance on self-evaluation

This *Handbook* applies to the inspection of schools in England from January 2000

London: The Stationery Office

ISBN 0 11 350111 0

Inspection Quality Division
Office for Standards in Education
Alexandra House
33 Kingsway
London WC2B 6SE

Telephone: 020 7421 6800
Website: http://www.ofsted.gov.uk

CONTENTS

INTRODUCTION

This Handbook *is published by Her Majesty's Chief Inspector of Schools (HMCI) for use by inspectors of special schools and pupil referral units (PRUs). Like earlier editions, the* Handbook *will also prove useful for school self-evaluation.*

The *Handbook* has been fully revised. It incorporates the requirements of the differentiated inspection system, in which the most effective schools are offered less intensive inspections than the rest. Both types of inspection lead to summary reports for parents, written to the same standard format, which form part of the longer reports.

The *Handbook* has three parts:

Part 1. Guidance on using the *Evaluation Schedule*
This presents the schedule for evaluating school effectiveness, which contains criteria or benchmarks against which schools can be gauged, together with guidance on collecting and weighing evidence to arrive at judgements.

Part 2. Guidance for inspectors on conducting inspections and writing reports

Part 3. Using the *Handbook* for school self-evaluation

INSPECTION

The *Handbook* shows how the inspection Framework, *Inspecting Schools*, should be applied in the inspection of special schools and PRUs. However, the central principles for recognising and judging the quality and standards of schools apply broadly to schools of all types and sizes. References to **school** in this *Handbook* generally apply also to **unit**, unless otherwise specified.

Registered inspectors will need to be aware when inspecting independent schools approved under section 347(i) of the Education Act 1996 that these schools are not subject to the same mandatory requirements as other special schools. The requirements for these schools are set out in regulations and guidance for independent schools, available from the DfEE. Likewise, registered inspectors will need to keep up to date with information from the DfEE about the 'approved arrangements' (including those for residential provision) for special schools.

The guidance in this *Handbook* is intended to help ensure that the inspection process is of the highest quality and that judgements about a school are both fair and rigorous. A good inspection is one where:

■ judgements about the educational standards achieved at the school and the strengths and weaknesses in teaching and other aspects are secured by sufficient valid and reliable evidence;

■ the main findings, summarised at the front of the inspection report, together with issues which the school should address in order to improve, are clearly identified and reported to the school.

It is equally important that:

- inspectors establish an effective working relationship with the school based on professionalism, sensitivity and an understanding of the school's concerns and circumstances;

- the process is well planned and effectively managed;

- there are good communications with the school and individual staff, which lead to a clear and shared understanding of what is involved at each stage of the inspection;

- inspectors readily explore issues with staff through professional dialogue;

- feedback to the school, staff and the governing body or appropriate authority, both orally and in writing, is clear and comprehensible.

Inspectors should leave the staff and members of the appropriate authority feeling that they have gained from their contact with the members of the team, as well as recognising the thoroughness of the evidence base and understanding and respecting the judgements which emerge. Those involved in running the school should feel that the inspection has provided a valuable contribution to their strategy for improvement.

The new system applies from January 2000.

SHORT AND FULL INSPECTIONS

This *Handbook* describes a differentiated inspection system. The aim is to offer the most effective schools a SHORT INSPECTION. Other schools and all PRUs will have a FULL INSPECTION, which resembles the inspections carried out to the previous Framework. This differentiated inspection system reflects the Government's commitment to less intervention in schools which are more successful.

Similarities and differences

SHORT and FULL INSPECTIONS have many common features. Both must:

- report on the quality of education provided by the school; the educational standards achieved by pupils in the school; the efficiency with which the financial resources available to the school are managed; and the spiritual, moral, social and cultural development of pupils at the school;

- result in an inspection report for the appropriate authority for the school, and a summary of the report for parents, written to a standard format;

- be conducted by inspection teams led by a registered inspector and include a lay inspector;

- use similar procedures before and after the inspection;

- continue to identify schools requiring special measures or having serious weaknesses, and report if a school is underachieving.

The differences in the two types of inspection are that:

■ only the FULL INSPECTION will lead to detailed reporting of each subject;

■ the FULL INSPECTION needs to fulfil the requirements of the whole *Evaluation Schedule*, but the SHORT INSPECTION may omit some parts;

■ feedback is offered to every member of staff during or at the end of FULL INSPECTIONS, but this is only done as far as is practicable, after lessons, in SHORT INSPECTIONS;

■ teachers are provided with a profile of their inspectors' judgements on their lessons after FULL, but not SHORT, INSPECTIONS;

■ the SHORT INSPECTION will not necessarily cover the work of every teacher.

The purpose and nature of a SHORT INSPECTION

The SHORT INSPECTION provides an educational 'health check' of the school. The inspection samples the school's work rather than inspecting and reporting fully on each subject. In all but the smallest schools, fewer inspectors will spend fewer days in the school than in a FULL INSPECTION. A SHORT INSPECTION usually lasts for two or three days, whereas a typical FULL INSPECTION lasts for up to a week. The team normally consists of between 2 and 5 inspectors for a SHORT INSPECTION. Although a SHORT INSPECTION will normally endorse the quality and standards of an effective school, it may sometimes find that a school is underachieving, has serious weaknesses or even requires special measures. This will mean that it is likely to be subject to HMI monitoring and/or an early FULL re-inspection. The report from a SHORT INSPECTION will focus selectively on the school's strengths and areas where improvement is needed. SHORT INSPECTIONS should cause less pressure on the school because the number of lessons observed is considerably smaller than in a FULL INSPECTION.

The purpose and nature of a FULL INSPECTION

The FULL INSPECTION provides an evaluation of the entire school. This includes inspection and reporting of the main subjects of the curriculum by inspectors who have specialist knowledge of those subjects. The FULL INSPECTION leads to a report on every aspect of the school listed in the *Evaluation Schedule*, except where particular aspects do not apply in the school or PRU concerned. In PRUs, Part D of the report (The standards and quality of teaching in areas of the curriculum, subjects and courses) is not required.

Part 1 of the *Handbook* provides guidance on using and interpreting the *Schedule*. All inspectors must be familiar with this guidance. Registered inspectors must ensure that members of their teams who carry responsibility for the inspection of particular aspects of the school thoroughly understand and use the guidance that applies to these aspects. The guidance must be interpreted sensibly during an actual inspection; some parts will be more relevant than others to the inspection of a particular school. It is for the registered inspector to judge where the priorities lie and how best to use the time available.

Part 2 of the *Handbook* provides guidance on how to conduct inspections and write reports. The registered inspector must comply with this guidance and ensure that members of the team also observe it.

SCHOOL MONITORING AND SELF-EVALUATION

The criteria in the *Evaluation Schedule* provide a secure basis for school self-evaluation. OFSTED is committed to promoting self-evaluation as a key aspect of the work of schools. Monitoring and evaluation are essential if the school is to set priorities and decide the action to take to improve the school's quality and raise the achievements of its pupils.

OFSTED has already made three substantial contributions to self-evaluation by:

i.   publishing *School Evaluation Matters* which was issued to all schools;

ii. preparing annual *Performance and Assessment (PANDA) reports* for all schools, apart from PRUs;

iii. developing a pack for training school evaluators.

Part 3 of the *Handbook* provides schools with advice on how to make use of the *Evaluation Schedule* for their own evaluation.

PART 1

GUIDANCE ON USING THE EVALUATION SCHEDULE

Part 1 provides guidance for all inspectors and school evaluators on the use
of the *Evaluation Schedule* which is set out in the Framework, *Inspecting Schools*.
The *Schedule* helps you to find the answers to a set of eight questions about a school.

THE STRUCTURE OF THE EVALUATION SCHEDULE

The *Schedule* is arranged in a way which both reflects the evaluation sequence and defines the summary of the inspection report (*see Figure 1*). It highlights the distinction between the **standards** achieved by pupils at the school, or outcomes, and the factors which contribute to these outcomes, **provision**, particularly the quality of teaching, and **leadership and management**. In using each section of the *Schedule*, you should have regard for what is achieved by, and provided for, *all* pupils in the school, whatever their age, attainment, gender, background, ethnicity or special educational need.

Figure 1: Structure of the Evaluation Schedule

CONTEXT AND OVERVIEW

1. **What sort of school is it?**

OUTCOMES

2. **How high are standards?**

    2.1 The school's results and pupils' achievements

    2.2 Pupils' attitudes, values and personal development

QUALITY OF PROVISION

3. **How well are pupils or students taught?**

    4. How good are the curricular and other opportunities offered to pupils or students?

    5. How well does the school care for its pupils or students?

    6. How well does the school work in partnership with parents?

EFFICIENCY AND EFFECTIVENESS OF MANAGEMENT

7. **How well is the school led and managed?**

ISSUES FOR THE SCHOOL

8. **What should the school do to improve further?**

CONTEXT AND OVERVIEW

■ *What sort of school is it?* This section describes the school, summarises its quality and standards, outlines strengths and weaknesses and evaluates improvement since the last inspection.

OUTCOMES

■ *How high are standards?* This question is covered in one section, with two areas of enquiry.

- Evaluation of *the school's results and achievements* should focus on the school's results; trends in performance; strengths and weaknesses in particular subjects. This is critical in PRUs where there is no requirement to report separately on subjects. You should also judge how well the pupils achieve, that is, whether *these* pupils in *this* school are getting on as well as they should.

- The section on *pupils' attitudes, values and personal development* explores pupils' response to the school: their attitudes; behaviour; personal development and relationships; and attendance.

QUALITY OF PROVISION

This is covered in four sections, the first of which is particularly important.

■ *How well are pupils or students taught?* This question requires you to look at the quality of teaching and learning. At the heart of the criteria is the extent to which pupils are challenged and engaged in learning, and are learning at the right level.

■ *How good are the curricular and other opportunities offered to pupils or students?* This question is concerned with the quality and range of the curriculum, including provision for pupils' spiritual, moral, social and cultural development, and extra-curricular provision including study support.

■ *How well does the school care for its pupils or students?* This question focuses, in SHORT INSPECTIONS, on the active steps the school takes to ensure pupils' welfare, health and safety, and in FULL INSPECTIONS on the overall assessment, support and guidance arrangements.

■ *How well does the school work in partnership with parents?* This question examines parents' views of the school and the basis for these views and, in FULL INSPECTIONS, the range of parental involvement in, and links with, the school.

EFFICIENCY AND EFFECTIVENESS OF MANAGEMENT

Effective schools invariably have a clear sense of purpose, drive and direction, supported by efficient and effective management and administration.

■ *How well is the school led and managed?* This question covers a range of enquiries into leadership, management, in particular, approaches to enhancing the performance, staffing and pupils; the role of governors and, in FULL INSPECTIONS, detailed questions about staffing, accommodation and resources.

THE STRUCTURE OF THE GUIDANCE ON USING THE EVALUATION SCHEDULE

Each section of the guidance includes the following five elements:

- The page from the *Evaluation Schedule* as in the Framework, *Inspecting Schools*;

- *Inspection focus*, which amplifies the main evaluation and reporting requirements, stressing the features on which an evaluation must concentrate;

- *Making judgements*, which provides guidance on where to pitch your evaluations, drawing from, but not re-stating, the criteria;

- *Reporting requirements*, which spells out what is expected in the reports of SHORT and FULL INSPECTIONS. The summary of the report follows the same format in both;

- *Guidance on using the criteria*, which illustrates how you should interpret the criteria and test the evidence against them. The criteria amount to a set of standards representing good practice. They provide a basis for accurate and consistent evaluation and for the identification of strengths and weaknesses. In reaching overall judgements, *all* the relevant criteria should be considered.

You should use the *Guidance on using the criteria* as a source of reference. In using the guidance, you must focus on the central judgements required by the Framework and not pursue such a diverse range of issues that the inspection becomes unmanageable.

When reporting, you should avoid quoting criteria verbatim and should concentrate on the reporting requirements highlighted in the *Evaluation Schedule*. You must draw evidence into the report in order to illustrate or explain judgements, bring the report to life, and capture the individual characteristics of the school.

USING THE *EVALUATION SCHEDULE* ON SHORT AND FULL INSPECTIONS

The *Schedule* maps out the lines of enquiry for the evaluation of schools. In FULL INSPECTIONS, the school must be evaluated and reported on in terms of all elements of the *Schedule*. In SHORT INSPECTIONS, those elements enclosed in a box are not required. The reporting requirements are indicated by a hollow square (☐).

1. WHAT SORT OF SCHOOL IS IT?

Inspectors must report on:

☐ the characteristics of the school;

and evaluate and summarise:

☐ the effectiveness of the school, including the value for money it provides;

☐ the main strengths and weaknesses of the school;

☐ the extent to which the school has improved, or not, since the last inspection;

relating their findings to the specific nature of the school and its pupils.

INSPECTION FOCUS

The inspection report for both SHORT and FULL INSPECTIONS must capture, as succinctly as possible, at the beginning of the summary:

■ the main features or characteristics that describe the school;

■ your overall view of its effectiveness, particularly in terms of its standards and quality of provision, and the value for money it provides.

After these two opening paragraphs, the report must list:

■ the strengths and weaknesses of the school, set out as WHAT THE SCHOOL DOES WELL and WHAT COULD BE IMPROVED.

After analysing any changes in the school's performance since the last inspection, the report should state:

■ the extent to which the school has improved, or not, since its last inspection;

giving reasons for this judgement.

Only the first of these four elements, the characteristics of the school, is known before the inspection. The other three are summative judgements, decided corporately, normally at the final meeting of the inspection team.

MAKING JUDGEMENTS

☐ The characteristics of the school

The report must start by giving the size, type and nature of the school. It should describe the background and circumstances of pupils who attend the school, their ethnic background, special educational needs and their attainment on entry. Additionally, you should mention other factors that may be relevant to the school's performance, for example, changing patterns of admissions to the school or unit.

Example 1.1

Extract from the summary of a report

High Down is a school for 73 pupils aged under 5 to post-16, with severe or profound and multiple learning difficulties. Currently, approximately 11 of the pupils have profound and multiple learning difficulties or additional physical or sensory impairments. Eight are identified as being autistic and six have behavioural difficulties. The majority of pupils have language and communication difficulties. Four of the children in the under-5s class attend the school on a part-time basis. Few pupils are from minority ethnic backgrounds.

The following table (*see Figure 2*) alerts you to the main points you need to consider when preparing your *Pre-Inspection Commentary* and planning the opening paragraph, INFORMATION ABOUT THE SCHOOL section, of the summary of the inspection report. The questions and prompts will be more relevant to some schools than others. You must use your judgement when deciding what to include in the full report. You should be guided by whether the information you include is relevant to the quality and standards of the school, and whether it is essential for current and prospective parents.

Figure 2: The characteristics of the school

Is it like other schools?	Refer as appropriate to: • number and age range of pupils; • gender of intake and significant gender imbalance; • type and category; • range of disabilities or need which the school/PRU provides; • approved arrangements, including residential provision (special schools) and agreed admission number (PRUs).
What is known of pupils' attainment on entry?	Note any: • variations in the attainment of pupils on entry, and over time.
Does it have a specific designation?	Is the school designated, for example, as: • a 'centre of excellence' or 'beacon school'; • part of an Education Action Zone (EAZ), 'Excellence in Cities' or other group (*see Annex 4*); • regional specialist provision?
Where is the school located and to what extent does the intake reflect the school's location?	Consider the school's context in relation to: • the background of its pupils; • whether the school serves its immediate area; • recent patterns of admission and transfer.
What is the proportion of pupils eligible for free schools meals?	Note: • how these compare with levels nationally and with similar types of schools (if known); • any trends with successive intakes.
What different groups are there in the school?	Note the numbers of: • pupils under 6 and if they are in nursery, reception or mixed-age classes; • ethnic groups represented in the school in significant numbers, including refugee children and asylum seekers; • Traveller children; • pupils for whom English is an additional language (EAL) and number of EAL pupils who are at the early stages of learning English; • pupils with different special educational needs; • other identifiable groups, for example non-attending pupils and recently admitted pupils.

☐ The effectiveness of the school

At the end of the inspection you need to summarise the team's view of how good the school is. You should substantiate this judgement, particularly in terms of the *standards* achieved by pupils by the time they leave, the quality of education, particularly *teaching*, the *leadership and management* of the school, and the extent to which it is improving. The **overall effectiveness** of the school is reported in the summary of the report, together with a comment on the *value for money* it provides (*see page 15*).

To reach a judgement about overall effectiveness, therefore, you will need to weigh up carefully the team's conclusions about the following indicators of effectiveness:

■ how well pupils achieve, and their attitudes, values and personal development;

■ the quality of education provided, particularly teaching;

■ how well the school is led and managed;

■ how far the school has improved or maintained very high standards since the last inspection.

In coming to your conclusions, you will need to take account of the characteristics of the school and the background of its pupils. You may find it helpful to collect together the team's corporate judgements which you have recorded in the *Record of Corporate Judgements* and place them on a table such as that below. You will give due weight to each area, giving particular attention to how well pupils achieve.

Figure 3: Aid to judging effectiveness

Judgement recording grade		1	2	3	4	5	6	7	
STANDARDS Pupils' achievements are:	Excellent	★	★	★	★	★	★	★	Very poor
Attitudes, values and personal development are:	Excellent	★	★	★	★	★	★	★	Very poor
PROVISION The quality of education, particularly teaching, is:	Excellent	★	★	★	★	★	★	★	Very poor
LEADERSHIP AND MANAGEMENT Leadership and management are:	Excellent	★	★	★	★	★	★	★	Very poor
IMPROVEMENT Improvement or maintenance of very high standards is:	Excellent	★	★	★	★	★	★	★	Very poor
CONTEXTUAL FACTORS The context of school in the local environment is:	Very unfavourable ★	★	★	★	★	★	★		Very favourable
EFFECTIVENESS The overall effectiveness of the school is:	Excellent	★	★	★	★	★	★	★	Very poor

The following characteristics illustrate where to pitch judgements about the overall effectiveness of the school or unit, but will vary according to the type of pupils.

Very good or excellent	The school achieves the highest standards possible in most of its work. Pupils have positive attitudes and are keen to be independent. Staff tackle individual problems, such as behaviour, very effectively. The teaching is consistently good, with much that is very good; and virtually all pupils achieve as much as they can. The staff constantly look for ways to improve the quality of their teaching, are imaginative and make challenging demands of pupils. There are very good arrangements to support all pupils and care for them, and the school has a strong partnership with parents and carers and outside agencies. The school is well managed and self-critical. It knows what it does well, where its weaknesses are and how to improve them. It has made significant improvement since its last inspection or has sustained high standards. It provides good or very good value for money.
Satisfactory or better	The school achieves standards that are at least as good as they should be, for the pupils it serves. Almost all the teaching is at least satisfactory and much is good or better, and pupils are learning well. Most of the pupils are on course to achieve their targets. The school has developed a curriculum that meets the needs of individual pupils and provides opportunities which benefit all pupils. There are sound care arrangements. The school keeps parents and carers informed about their child's progress and enlists their support and that of outside agencies. The school has made satisfactory improvement since its last inspection and responds adequately to the challenges or issues it faces. It is inclusive in its policies, outlook and practices. It is well led and is managed efficiently, providing satisfactory value for money.

However, if the judgement is that the school is **not as effective as it should be, poor or very poor**, then you must consider as a team:

- whether or not the **school is failing, or likely to fail, to give its pupils an acceptable standard of education, and thus requires special measures**;

- whether or not **the school, although providing an acceptable standard of education,** nevertheless **has serious weaknesses in one or more areas of its work**;

- whether **the school, although not identified as having serious weakness, is judged to be under-achieving.**

Any of these findings must always be *stated explicitly in the report* **using the form of words highlighted above** (*see Annex 2*).

Example 1.2

Extract from the summary of a report on an MLD school

The school provides a high standard of teaching and care for its pupils. Almost all the pupils and students gain the crucial skills of literacy and numeracy, and communicate well. The ethos of the school is excellent. The school makes very good provision for the support, guidance and welfare of pupils and for their spiritual, social, moral and cultural development. It gives very good value for money.

[Overall: a very good school (2)]

Judging value for money

The value for money provided by the school is a composite assessment of its effectiveness and efficiency in relation to its costs. You can only make this judgement when you have considered all the other elements of the inspection.

In schools or units which do not have a fully delegated budget, or where you have little information about how unit costs compare with similar establishments, the following procedures will not apply. You should, however, judge the cost-effectiveness of what is provided. You should take account, for example, of the appropriateness of spending decisions, whether staff are deployed in the most effective way, and the quality and impact of any special facilities or support.

Your judgements should be based on a careful weighing up of the team's conclusions about:

■ the overall effectiveness of the school;

taking into account the characteristics of the school and the background of its pupils.

You should then relate these evaluations to:

■ the unit costs of the school and its cost-effectiveness;

taking account of the efficiency with which the school is run.

In broad terms, you should consider value for money as effectiveness set against costs, and this can be illustrated in a two-way table.

Figure 4: Value for money as effectiveness set against cost

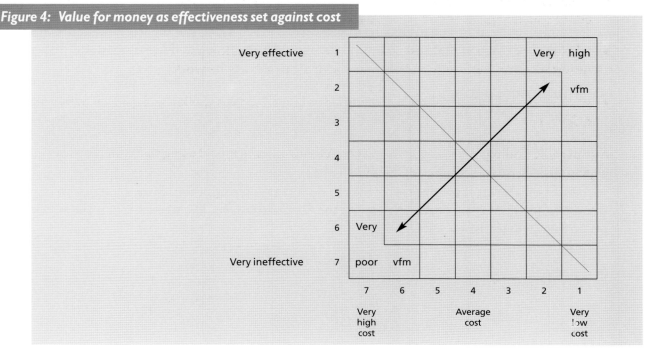

Put another way, you should consider the main judgement recording statement for the overall effectiveness of the school alongside contextual factors and the school's expenditure per pupil.

Judgement recording grade		1	2	3	4	5	6	7	
EFFECTIVENESS The overall effectiveness of the school:	Excellent	★	★	★	★	★	★	★	Very poor
CONTEXTUAL FACTORS The school and its pupils in the local environment:	Very favourable	★	★	★	★	★	★	★	Very unfavourable
UNIT COSTS The school's expenditure per pupil:	Very low	★	★	★	★	★	★	★	Very high
VALUE FOR MONEY The value for money provided by the school:	Excellent	★	★	★	★	★	★	★	Very poor

Example 1.3

Extract from a report of a pupil referral unit

Although overall the pupils at the unit make sound progress, improve their behaviour and develop satisfactory attitudes to their work, their attendance is poor and personal development unsatisfactory. The quality of teaching is satisfactory, but the half-time schooling limits what is taught and the progress pupils can make. There are also weaknesses in the management and monitoring of pupils' individual education plans and programmes, and the generous ratio of adult staff to pupils is not used effectively. Taking these factors into account, with the current high unit cost per pupil, the unit gives unsatisfactory value for money.

☐ The main strengths and weaknesses of the school

At its final meeting, the team must corporately decide which aspects of the school are particularly good and which aspects are weak, if any. These should be recorded in the sections of the inspection report headed:

WHAT THE SCHOOL DOES WELL

and

WHAT COULD BE IMPROVED

The balance between these strengths and areas for improvement should reflect the overall quality of the school. The areas for improvement should form the basis for the issues for action to improve standards and quality set out in section 8 of the *Evaluation Schedule*, WHAT SHOULD THE SCHOOL DO TO IMPROVE FURTHER?

☐ The extent to which the school has improved, or not, since the last inspection

Your evaluation of the school's current performance and your analysis of how the school has changed since its last inspection is integral to your judgement about its improvement. By the end of the inspection you must be able to report on how much improvement has been made and judge whether it has been enough. This overall judgement must relate to:

- how much change could reasonably be expected;

- what the school has done and if it has been enough.

You must give reasons for the overall judgement, drawing on illustrative evidence from different sections of the report. This should normally include, for example:

- improved performance in National Curriculum tests and tasks, if applicable;

- increasing numbers of pupils achieving success in nationally or locally accredited courses or moving into further and higher education, or, where appropriate, returning to mainstream schooling;

- improvements in the quality of teaching and pupils' learning;

- how well the school's leadership has responded to the previous inspection, and what it has done to improve or maintain high standards and increase the cost-effectiveness of its provision.

Example 1.4

Extract from the summary of a report on a school for pupils with severe learning difficulties of secondary age

The school has overcome most of the weaknesses identified in the last inspection. It now provides a balanced curriculum in which all subjects are well established, with effective schemes of work and assessment schedules. Individual education plans have been improved dramatically and their constant use has undoubtedly contributed to the higher standards in English, mathematics and science, and in locally validated accreditation schemes. Statements are now reviewed more systematically, and both parents and the careers service are much more closely involved.

[Overall: very good improvement (2)]

How much change could reasonably be expected?

The previous report indicated what improvements were needed. The school may also have identified its own areas for improvement. You will need to consider the improvement made in relation to the school's own targets, and any changes in the characteristics of the pupils who attend the school. A few schools will have done well to maintain very high standards or sustain the exceptional quality of what they provide. For all schools there is an expectation of either continued improvement or sustained excellence.

For FULL INSPECTIONS, each section of the commentary and each subject section should refer to the extent of improvement in the areas or subjects concerned, as applicable. In particular, you must consider standards, teaching and leadership and management as well as the school's ethos in making your judgement.

The threshold for **expected** ('satisfactory') **improvement** is illustrated by the presence of many of the following features:

In terms of the **standards achieved,** there is evidence of:

■ substantial improvement in attendance, attitudes and behaviour of pupils, if these were poor or unsatisfactory;

■ improved rates of academic progress, particularly in communication skills and numeracy, and improvements in pupils' personal development;

■ as many pupils as possible working towards accredited awards.

In terms of the **quality of education provided,** there is evidence of:

■ improved teaching in the areas where it was weakest, particularly if it affected expectations, subject expertise and knowledge of pupils' disabilities in supporting their learning and managing difficult behaviour;

■ the school providing a wider range of curricular opportunities such as a modern foreign language, work experience or vocational courses which are robust enough to survive staff changes;

■ a successful effort to consider and redress other areas of weakness identified in the previous report;

■ effective action on the main key issues, particularly those related to standards;

■ evidence that the school has monitored its progress.

In **leadership and management,** there is evidence of:

■ improved admissions procedures within the framework of criteria for admissions set by the LEA;

■ resources and expertise being directed towards priorities related to raising standards, for example more effectively deploying learning support assistants;

■ development of self-evaluation, particularly reviewing individual targets to assess whether they are sufficiently challenging.

In relation to the **ethos** of the school, there is evidence that weaknesses have been overcome and there is:

■ general staff commitment to the achievement of high standards;

■ pupil and parent satisfaction;

■ good working relationships across the school.

What the school has done and has it been enough?

In making this judgement you will need to give greatest weight to any changes in the standards achieved by pupils, the quality of teaching, leadership and how the school is managed. The weighting you give to other changes will depend on the impact they have on pupils' progress and achievements.

Illustrate your judgement to show how change has been brought about. Reasons for change might include:

- effective action planning;

- the appointment of a new headteacher or other key staff;

- the school's ability to identify and deal effectively with its own weaknesses.

The appropriate authority is not obliged to address a key issue, but where it has not, it should have a convincing reason.

If you decide that the improvement has not been good enough, you will need to consider whether the school has serious weaknesses in one or more areas, or requires special measures to help it to improve.

Example 1.5

Extract from the summary of a report (PMLD)

Since the last inspection, the school has responded to some of the more tractable key issues from the last report. Little has been done, however, to raise the quality of teaching, which is still unfocused in too many lessons. Few pupils have specific targets for attainment, and planning remains weak. Special support staff are largely unaware of the educational intentions for some of the pupils they work with. Senior management is complacent, and pupils are achieving markedly less than they could.

[Overall: very little improvement, school requires special measures (7)]

Example 1.6 illustrates how the first five sections of the summary report might appear when completed in the way described in this section.

Example 1.6 Summary of the inspection report

ST JOHN'S SCHOOL
[location including main post town]
Headteacher: [name]
Date of inspection: [start – end date]

Four inspectors, led by [name of registered inspector] inspected the school. This is a summary of the full inspection report, which is available from the school.

INFORMATION ABOUT THE SCHOOL

St John's is a maintained special school for pupils aged 11–19 who have severe, profound and multiple learning difficulties (PMLD). It is approved for 65 pupils and has 60 pupils on roll with just over a third of pupils with PMLD, similar to many other schools nationally. Half the pupils are from minority ethnic backgrounds, much higher than is normally found but reflecting the community it serves. Just less than half the pupils are entitled to free school meals, which is high in comparison with most schools. All pupils have statements of special educational needs.

HOW GOOD THE SCHOOL IS

St John's is an effective school with good provision to meet the needs of most pupils. By the time the students leave to go into further education or employment they achieve well, gaining external accreditation for their work, which the local college and employers value. This reflects on the consistently good teaching and a very well-planned curriculum. Governors work conscientiously and very closely with staff to identify areas to improve. The school provides satisfactory value for money.

WHAT THE SCHOOL DOES WELL

- Students at 19 achieve well in all their work and all gain external qualifications
- The majority of pupils make good progress in speaking and listening, supported well by signing which is effectively and consistently taught
- All pupils have very good attitudes to the work and put much effort into their learning
- Relationships are excellent and behaviour in and out of school is exemplary
- Teaching is very good for pupils aged 14–16 and work with students post-16 is challenging
- Pupils' work in art and music is very good throughout the school
- The headteacher, supported by senior staff, leads the school well; the governors are well informed about the work of the school, and have a clear plan for future improvement

WHAT COULD BE IMPROVED

- The provision of more resources and support to boost the achievement of PMLD pupils
- Teaching of science and mathematics for pupils aged 11–14, ensuring that the work is well planned and interests pupils more
- Provision for information and communications technology, to enable more pupils to make use of computers to aid their learning
- The use of learning support assistants, to provide more groups with the help they need

The areas for improvement will form the basis of the governors' action plan.

HOW THE SCHOOL HAS IMPROVED SINCE ITS LAST INSPECTION

The school has made good progress in dealing with weaknesses identified in the last inspection in May 1996. There is significant improvement in the teaching of communication skills and signing is now taught much more consistently. The curriculum is broad and balanced and now includes work in history and geography. The allocation of time to different subjects is more even, helped by an increase in teaching time, so that work throughout the school is better balanced.

2. HOW HIGH ARE STANDARDS?

2.1 THE SCHOOL'S RESULTS AND PUPILS' ACHIEVEMENTS

Inspectors must *interpret* and report on:

☐ the school's results and other performance data at the end of each stage of education, particularly in English, mathematics and science, highlighting any variations of achievement by different groups of pupils and in different subjects;

☐ trends in results over time;

☐ the school's progress towards its targets, including comment on whether the targets are sufficiently challenging.

Inspectors must *evaluate* and report on:

☐ standards of work seen, emphasising literacy and numeracy, and highlighting strengths and weaknesses in what pupils know, understand and can do;

- all the subjects inspected, focusing on the work of the oldest pupils at each stage;
- the variations between different groups of pupils and between subjects;

☐ how well pupils achieve, taking account of the progress they have made, the level of demand placed on them and other relevant factors.

In determining their judgements, inspectors should consider, where relevant, the extent to which:

- the results in National Curriculum and other tests, examinations and accreditations match or exceed the average for all schools;

- children under 5 years are likely to attain or do better than the expected goals or standards by the time they start Year 1;

- the school is either maintaining very high standards or improving as expected;

- the school sets challenging targets and is on course to meet or exceed them;

- pupils with special educational needs, having English as an additional language or who are gifted and talented, are making good progress;

- standards are consistently high across subjects;

- there are no significant differences in the standards achieved by pupils of different gender or ethnic background;

- results in the school are high compared with those of similar schools (or show significant added value in relation to pupils' earlier results);

- pupils' attainment meet or exceed the levels set by: the National Curriculum and, where applicable; the local agreed syllabus for religious education; any examination or assessment objectives.

INSPECTION FOCUS

The inspection report must say clearly what pupils at the school or unit achieve and whether this is as much as it could or should be, giving reasons for these findings. This requirement applies to the inspection of all special schools and pupil referral units. You must interpret this, however, in a way which reflects the type of school or unit and the needs, disabilities or challenges of the pupils for whom it provides.

Where schools enter pupils for external tests, examinations or other forms of accreditation, you must also report on and interpret these results to parents, indicating the standards reached at different stages and, particularly by the time pupils leave.

In this guidance we use the word *standards* to denote the attainment of pupils in relation to a clear benchmark, such as National Curriculum levels or descriptions at the end of a Key Stage. Some pupils in special schools, despite a particular disability, achieve standards which are comparable to, or in some cases higher than, their peers in mainstream schools. Many other pupils, having different degrees of difficulty with learning, nevertheless attain particular levels in National Curriculum subjects or grades in GCSE examinations or other accredited courses. When reporting on such results, you should indicate what levels of competence they reflect, particularly in the skills of English and mathematics.

You must always evaluate the *achievement* of pupils in special schools and pupil referral units. Achievement reflects the accomplishments of pupils in relation to what you would expect of those particular pupils. Pupils' statements, individual education plans and targets, and annual reviews provide indispensable reference points against which to gauge progress and judge current achievement. You should judge achievement by applying insight and expertise to all the evidence you have about the pupils, taking account of: where they have come from in terms of prior attainment; what they know, understand and can do; what they are being asked to do; and what targets have been set.

Your judgements should be linked to other parts of the report and with your appraisal of what the school is doing to maximise pupils' achievement, particularly in terms of the quality of teaching and other support for learning. The way in which this section of the report is constructed will depend on the type and nature of the special school or PRU.

Evidence of achievement and whether it is as high as possible comes, therefore, from three main sources:

i.   direct observation and examination of what pupils know, understand and can do;

ii.   the progress pupils have made, judged over a period of at least 12 months or, particularly in the case of PRUs, since admission. Your judgements must include a representative sample of the oldest pupils in SHORT INSPECTIONS of special schools and reflect pupils in each key stage on FULL INSPECTIONS. Make sure your judgements are based on a sample which is representative of the different groups of pupils in the school in terms of age, gender, disability and time since admission;

iii.   the learning demands made of pupils and their response to these.

In judging achievement, in both special schools and PRUs, you must give priority to English, mathematics, and personal, social and health education and other academic targets set at annual reviews or in individual education plans (IEPs).

You should always bear in mind the special circumstances of the school, and the impact the special needs have on pupils' achievement, so that your judgements are fair as well as rigorous. The achievement of any group of pupils is judged by the same criteria, which must be applied with sensitivity and awareness of what can reasonably be expected of the pupils.

In both special schools and in PRUs, your enquiries in relation to achievement will focus on the school's records of pupils' success in achieving their individual targets set and reviewed by teacher assessment, and by externally moderated assessment of achievement.

Sometimes, targets for groups of pupils will be set and this evidence must also be scrutinised. You must also make your own observations of pupils' achievements in lessons to validate or otherwise what you find from the records. Your task is to find how well pupils are achieving, whether pupils are making progress at a fast enough rate, and if the school is adding value.

MAKING JUDGEMENTS

Your judgements will rely on your own observations of pupils during the inspection and what you find out about what they know, understand and can do, and how well they are learning in lessons. These judgements should be validated by your interpretation and analysis of the records of individual pupils, their achievements in relation to their academic targets, and their progress towards them.

You should also ensure that your judgements of achievement:

- take account of important milestones such as improved communication, literacy or numeracy skills or transfer to further education, training or work, or back to mainstream schools;

- reflect the progress made during each key stage or up to age 5 and between ages 16 and 19, and are consistent with your judgements on teaching and learning.

Example 2.1.1

Extract from a report of a special school

Achievements in English are good. Many pupils can hardly communicate when they start the nursery. By 6 or 7 most listen, make eye contact, use signing and speaking, and have developed some initial skills for reading and writing. Many can recognise and find their own photograph. Given a toy, some can select from a choice of photographs the one which matches the toy; some can also find the word for the object. Children with complex learning needs respond well to stimuli. In drama, when listening to a story about a walk in a wood, they listened to leaves crackling, felt the wind and the rain, smelt the fire and responded well to the enactment of poetry and prose. Some imitated the sounds of twigs snapping; others were engrossed in the feel of the spider's web.

[Overall: low attainment, but good achievement (3)]

The following characteristics illustrate where to pitch your judgements about *how well pupils achieve* in special schools and PRUs.

Very good or excellent achievement	Almost all pupils are achieving as well as they can. Pupils regularly succeed in meeting or surpassing the great majority of key targets across a range of subjects or areas of work, over at least a 12-month period. The targets are challenging and reviewed at regular intervals. Pupils have striking success in achieving a difficult target where sustained and prolonged work is necessary, as a step towards an important future milestone.
Sound or better achievement	The achievement of the majority of pupils is satisfactory, and they make steady progress in their learning. Pupils achieve, or are on course to achieve most (more than a half) of the key targets and lower priority targets, which relate to the whole range of a subject or area of work.

However, standards are **unlikely to be satisfactory**, if any of the following features are present:

- less than half the targets set are successfully achieved over a 12-month period or likely to be achieved, unless due to particular unforeseen medical conditions or other relevant factors;

- repetition of the same targets over a sustained period of time;

- lack of success in important aspects of a subject or area of learning;

- important and relevant milestones not reached;

- pupils are making little progress.

You must be flexible in interpreting this guidance, particularly in schools where there are pupils with regressive conditions, where the priority must be to ensure that their comfort, safety, dignity and overall well-being are safeguarded.

Your judgements on the standards achieved in English, mathematics, personal social and health education should be reported in the summary report using the appropriate letter A–E.

In all cases make sure you give reasons for your judgements and link these judgements to what you are finding in other aspects of the inspection, so that you provide a consistent message throughout the report. **Always** report on what pupils know, understand and can do to exemplify your judgements on achievement and **where possible and appropriate**, report attainment in relation to the early learning goals, the expected levels of the National Curriculum, or in relation to external courses or examinations.

REPORTING REQUIREMENTS

SUMMARY REPORT

On all inspections you must complete the table headed STANDARDS based on achievements in relation to individual targets and for English, mathematics, personal, social and health education (PSHE) (oldest pupils or students only for SHORT INSPECTIONS). You should make brief comments **where possible and appropriate** on how well pupils achieve in subjects taught, including examination or test results. For all special schools and PRUs, you should indicate where progress is particularly strong or weak in subjects taught. Reference should be made to trends in performance over time in relation to both school and individual targets.

If any of these are a feature of improvement in the school, record this in the section HOW THE SCHOOL HAS IMPROVED SINCE ITS LAST INSPECTION.

Any subjects or areas of work that are particularly good or need to improve must be reported under WHAT THE SCHOOL DOES WELL or WHAT COULD BE IMPROVED.

SHORT INSPECTIONS

Expand in the commentary any items featured in WHAT THE SCHOOL DOES WELL or WHAT COULD BE IMPROVED. Where applicable complete the data tables at the back of the report.

FULL INSPECTIONS

Report under the section headed HOW HIGH ARE STANDARDS? Where applicable, complete the tables at the back of the report.

GUIDANCE ON USING THE CRITERIA

☐ The school's results and other performance data

Do the school's results in National Curriculum and other tests, if applicable, match or exceed the average for all schools? Are children who are 5 years or under likely to attain, or do better than, the expected goals or standards by the time they start Year 1? To what extent do pupils' attainments meet or exceed the levels set by the National Curriculum, the local agreed syllabus for religious education, and any assessment objectives or individual targets?

Before the inspection, you should find out as much as possible about the nature and range of the intake of pupils in the special school or PRU, particularly the approved arrangements for special schools from the DfEE and agreed admission number for PRUs from the LEA. *Forms S1 and S2* will tell you about the characteristics and type of special school or PRU, the range of needs served and the age profile. You should start the inspection as clear as possible about the range of attainment you are likely to find during the inspection. In some special schools and PRUs, you may have available results of National Curriculum assessments or other examinations, which because the intake reflects the normal range of attainment, you can compare to all schools. In all special schools and PRUs you should have available the results of a range of externally accredited achievements or the records of achievement in relation to individual targets set in IEPs or at annual reviews. There are no *PICSI reports* for special schools or PRUs, but there is a *PICSI* annex for special schools, which contains national data for reference. Remember, as stated in the *PICSI* annex, 'there can be large variations between schools of the same type', so do not make comparisons with the national figures, unless you are sure of their validity.

Much of your work before the inspection is to arrange for the team **during the** inspection to have access to all the available evidence needed for judging the achievements of a representative sample of pupils (no less than 20 per cent) for each stage of the school (the oldest pupils only in SHORT INSPECTIONS). To do this, you must have evidence of pupils' prior attainment either on admission, in the case of PRUs, or at least 12 months ago in the case of special schools. You should make arrangements to find out what the school's procedures are for setting targets because an important prerequisite for judging progress is the effectiveness and challenge of the targets that are set. You should be clear about the function and role of the PRU and keep in mind that statutory requirements for implementing the National Curriculum and for its assessment do not apply. In the case of special schools use may be made of the permitted flexibility to teach the programmes of study of the National Curriculum according to developmental need.

For pupils under 5, information provided by the headteacher will help you to come to some initial views on what pupils know, understand and can do in relation to the Early Learning Goals. Similarly, for pupils at 5 years of age in the reception year, baseline data should be available. Use this information to prepare the team for the range of attainment that they might expect to see when directly observing pupils in lessons. These judgements will be needed later when making judgements on how much progress pupils have made.

In those special schools or PRUs **where it is appropriate** to compare the results of tests or examinations with the national averages, use the most recent results as a basis for comparison. You will **not** have a letter grade to compare standards to all schools nationally but you can report on the school's performance giving priority to English, mathematics, science in the summary report under the table 'Standards in subjects', as well as commenting in this section of the *Evaluation Schedule*.

You should, early on in the inspection, arrange to look at the sample of pupils' records, and, wherever possible, to discuss these with teachers, so that you can evaluate the range of attainment from the records, and also find out pupils' prior attainment. You will need to check that what is recorded tallies with what you observe of pupils' attainment in lessons. At this stage you can also ascertain how much more information you may need later in the inspection, for example through scrutiny of work, or videos or other kinds of records.

Find out from records and teachers' assessments:

■ how well pupils are attaining in speaking, listening, reading, writing and mathematics at 5 and at each Key Stage and by 19 years;

■ how well pupils are attaining within subjects, for example in reading compared with writing;

■ how well pupils are attaining in personal, social and health education at 5, each Key Stage and by 19 years;

■ how well pupils are attaining in one subject compared to another;

■ significant differences in attainment between boys and girls.

These data from the school's records, supplemented with what you find out in lessons on what pupils know, understand and can do, provide you with essential points of reference when you come to judge the progress pupils have made (see later guidance).

You must discuss with the headteacher of any school serving more than one significant minority ethnic group any other significant variation in attainment by different groups of pupils. A key indicator of the effectiveness of the school's management is the extent to which the school monitors and analyses performance to the extent indicated above, particularly in terms of minority groups.

For students aged 16 to 19, comment on the results of achievements which are externally moderated or accredited. In some instances, it may be the case that the results relate to the consequences of teaching elsewhere, for example, in a further education college or other community-based provision. You should indicate if these arrangements have a bearing on the results, particularly if there is marked disparity in achievements. For further guidance on inspecting advanced level courses, see the *Guidance on Inspecting Subjects 11–18*, published by OFSTED.

☐ Trends in results over time

Is the school either maintaining very high standards or improving as expected?

Comparative data on trends of improvement in special schools or PRUs will not be available to help you make your judgements. Bearing in mind recent, and in the case of PRUs, regular changes to the attainment profile, you should examine any performance trends, for example:

■ proportionately greater involvement and improved performance in National Curriculum tests or tasks;

■ increased success in communication skills (including literacy) and numeracy;

■ successful achievement of individual and school-based group targets;

■ increased numbers of pupils achieving success in externally accredited courses;

■ increased numbers of pupils moving on to further or higher education or back to mainstream schools, because of improved academic performance;

■ performance in any subject is persistently lower than the others;

■ any significant variation in performance by **particular groups of pupils, by age, ethnicity, gender or disability**.

Where relevant and appropriate, look to see if results of teacher assessments are broadly in line with the results of National Curriculum tests. If there are discrepancies this may point you to important factors such as low expectation or over-grading. Look for evidence that the teacher's assessment of attainment, particularly where are very small steps in progress, is moderated and validated by other colleagues.

When you visit the school before the inspection ask for evidence that the school analyses its assessments of pupils' work to identify strengths and weaknesses and to monitor the results of pupils from minority ethnic backgrounds and any other group; ask what action it takes to help particular groups of pupils, including those identified as having additional or complex special educational needs.

□ **The school's progress towards its targets**

Does the school set challenging targets and is it on course to meet or exceed them?

In special schools, target setting at Key Stages 2 and 4, based on National Curriculum test scores or examination results is likely to be found in only a relatively small number of schools. In some, for example, schools for pupils with emotional and behavioural difficulties the attainment profile may differ from year to year making trends of improvement less easy to discern because targets do not follow a linear pattern of improvement. Although not mandatory, you may find that targets are set in relation to a particular number of pupils achieving specified reading or numeracy skills or to achieve high levels of participation and success in externally accredited courses. For pupils with severe and profound and multiple learning difficulties, you may find that targets are set which relate to the numbers of pupils who attain levels which are prior to level 1, in line with recent national guidance.

In PRUs, targets are not mandatory although some units set these. Both in special schools and PRUs, evaluate how, despite fluctuating numbers and changing attainment profiles, the school by its careful assessment of pupils' achievements, sets challenging targets to ensure that all pupils do their best, and their achievements are recognised as a basis for judging the school's effectiveness. Find out how well the school collates and presents its results so that the results can be easily understood by those concerned, for example, parents, governors or management group; this information may also form the basis for reporting on the success of the school's SEN policy. Find out if the school has clearly analysed all the data to help it take the action necessary to make any improvements.

Look for evidence that the school has identified that particular groups of pupils are performing relatively less well than others.

See whether the school's interpretation of this data matches your own analysis. Whether it does or does not this will give you a valuable insight into the quality and rigour of the school's analysis of pupils' performance. It is reasonable to expect special schools and PRUs to have substantial data on individual pupil's performance, and for this data to be used as a basis for evaluating overall effectiveness.

To assess the effectiveness of the school's monitoring and its use of the findings to set targets for groups of pupils, you should check the accuracy of any baseline testing used prior to the target setting. In some special schools the LEA will be involved in helping the school.

Find out the rationale of particular targets set, say in communication skills, including reading, spelling or numeracy or in relation to externally accredited courses. See if they are realistic yet represent improvement from the baseline data. Much of this evidence will overlap with what you find out about individual target setting when you come to judge progress.

Find out the extent to which the school reflects on its own performance, has a realistic appreciation of its own strengths and weaknesses and of its own capacity to improve.

☐ Standards of work seen

In SHORT INSPECTIONS, special schools only, record what you can on what pupils know, understand and can do across the school, particularly the attainment of the oldest pupils.

In FULL INSPECTIONS only, you will need to undertake a more detailed evaluation of:

■ each subject inspected, focusing on a representative sample of pupils in each stage;

■ variations between the work of different groups of pupils and between different subjects.

For PRUs, note that there is no requirement to report separately on subjects elsewhere in the schedule.

Are standards consistently high across subjects?

You should plan carefully the best way to secure the evidence you need to evaluate what pupils know, understand and can do particularly in relation to the oldest pupils. You need to do this in liaison with the school. The range and extent of the evidence is much less on SHORT INSPECTIONS so you must identify what needs to be done at pre-inspection stage to make sure you capture essential evidence.

In FULL INSPECTIONS, you should find out what pupils know, understand and can do for each area of the curriculum or subject taught.

Whenever it is appropriate, indicate how the attainment compares to the expected levels of the early learning goals and to subjects of the National Curriculum and in relation to the locally agreed syllabus for RE.

In all cases evaluate relative strengths and weaknesses in what pupils know, understand and can do in relation to the Early Learning Goals and the programmes of study of the National Curriculum, which should act as your reference point to substantiate your judgements. For example if a pupil is relatively better at reading compared to writing, this should be noted. Give priority to speaking, listening, reading and writing and to mathematics and PSHE. You will need to check that your evaluation tallies with what is in the school records and reviews of individual targets. You should explain any disparities between what you observe and what is found in records.

Gather evidence by:

- observing and talking to pupils in lessons;

- listening to pupils asking and answering questions in plenary sessions;

- analysing the work they have produced;

- looking at records of attainment;

- questioning and talking to groups of pupils;

- talking to co-ordinators and looking at records together;

- looking at portfolios of 'levelled' work.

When you evaluate pupils' communication skills including literacy and numeracy, find out how well pupils use their skills in all subjects, or whether their understanding of important aspects of these subjects is hindered by poor skills.

On *Evidence Forms*, make sure you record pupils' strengths and weaknesses within and between subjects so that you can use this evidence to gauge and validate the school's records on the progress pupils make. Always provide grades in the section on attainment even if comparison with expected levels for the age is not reported.

You will need to use the evidence of what pupils know, understand and can do with your judgements about progress so as to make clear why the progress is as it is.

Where it is appropriate to judge attainment in relation to the levels expected for the age or in relation to the locally agreed syllabus, you will need to know the proportion of pupils who are on course to **achieve or exceed the expected goals by end of the reception year,** or **the expected levels in the National Curriculum at 7, 11, 14 and 16** or how results compare with national figures at 18, before you can make your judgements.

When appropriate, you should compare your judgements on standards in the core subjects with the results of end of Key Stage tests or other assessment data. If there are differences between your findings and the data, you should explain why this is so, making particular reference to what you find out about teaching and learning and the prior attainment and progress of the pupils in the school at the time of inspection.

Are pupils with special educational needs, those with English as an additional language or who are gifted or talented, making good progress? Are there significant differences in the standards achieved by pupils of different gender or ethnic backgrounds?

Throughout both SHORT and FULL INSPECTIONS you should make sure you focus on **how well different groups of pupils are performing.**

To help you judge the progress, where relevant, made by the **gifted and talented pupils** occasionally found in special schools, find out if the school uses its assessment data to identify and make provision for these pupils. If schools appear to have few high attainers, check from your observations of pupils' work in lessons, and by talking to pupils, whether the results and the school's assessment data accurately reflect pupils' aptitudes.

In schools where gifted and talented pupils are identified, be sure you gather sufficient evidence to judge whether their **progress is good enough**. In schools where gifted and talented pupils are present, but not adequately catered for, gather sufficient evidence to substantiate judgements about their underachievement.

To evaluate the **progress made by pupils for whom English is an additional language**, you should find out their competency in English by reference to the levels in the National Curriculum, as this will determine the kind of help they need. Gather sufficient evidence from lessons where these pupils are receiving support, or from any specialist teaching, so that you can make judgements on their progress. Make sure you record on *Evidence Forms* gains in all aspects of English to substantiate your judgements.

☐ How well do pupils achieve?

The most crucial judgement in this section of the *Evaluation Schedule* is whether pupils are achieving as much as they could and should. You already know from scrutiny of records and reviews of IEPs, discussions with teachers, therapists and learning support assistants and your own observations, what pupils know, understand and can do in each class you visit. (You will need to be aware that schools are not required to produce IEPs, but their use is recommended as good practice in the Code of Practice for SEN.)

In the absence of comparative data, your judgements about **achievement** are drawn from a composite of:

firsthand evidence

This comprises your focused observations of pupils in class, discussion with pupils and their teachers, and scrutinies of previous work wherever available. Here you are assessing the quality of their learning, what they are doing, what they have done, and what they can communicate about their work.

You should also take into account the nature and level of the demands made by teachers, the challenges pupils face, and their application.

assessments and records

Records should allow you to identify previous attainment and evaluate the rate at which particular pupils have progressed. You should consider the progress made over a period of at least 12 months by a representative sample of pupils identified before the inspection for each stage of the school, or in short inspections the oldest pupils. As with your judgements on attainment, give priority to English and mathematics and to personal, social and health education and other academic targets and IEPs or annual reviews.

The most useful include:

- teachers' daily records and assessments, and the records of attainment for each subject taught;

- records of attainment in IEPs or in annual reviews and reports to parents;

- video and photographic records;

- statements of special educational needs;

- information about attainment on admission and pupils' educational history.

related evidence

This may include: the quality and range of the curriculum, ensuring that attainment is judged across each subject taught; the quality and effectiveness of target setting, so as to ensure that targets are realistic, relevant and sufficiently rigorous; and the match between your direct observations of teaching and learning and the recorded assessments of pupils.

In the light of what you know about pupils' attainment from records and from your own observations, judge whether achievement **is sufficient** taking into account:

■ the impact on attainment of the special educational needs of the pupil;

■ prior attainment, attainment on admission and pupils' previous educational history;

■ any other relevant factors, such as the impact of medical conditions.

In making your judgements about achievement, you need to decide what weight to give to different kinds of evidence, including your observations of pupils in class. For example, in the case of pupils with severe learning difficulties, evidence of progress seen during the inspection in lessons will inevitably be limited, and you should give particular weight to the records and other evidence of achievement. In schools where record-keeping or target-setting is weak, you should take account of what you find out from discussions with teachers, what you see in lessons and where possible by close questioning of pupils about their work over time.

In relation to **target-setting**, you should judge whether targets:

■ are thought out in relation to long term goals and that careful consideration is given to the individual's particular needs;

■ are set to be achieved by a certain time with clear criteria for success;

■ are written clearly so that their success can be regularly assessed;

■ are realistic in relation to previous work;

■ take careful account of the pupil's performance in different contexts when setting new targets;

■ wherever possible involve pupils;

■ are agreed by parents;

■ are taxing but not impossible to achieve.

2.2 PUPILS' ATTITUDES, VALUES AND PERSONAL DEVELOPMENT

Inspectors must evaluate and report on pupils':

☐ attitudes to the school;

☐ behaviour, including the incidence of exclusions;

☐ personal development and relationships;

☐ attendance.

In determining their judgements, inspectors should consider the extent to which pupils:

• are keen and eager to come to school;

• show interest in school life, and are involved in the range of activities the school provides;

• behave well in lessons and around the school, are courteous, trustworthy and show respect for property;

• form constructive relationships with one another, and with teachers and other adults;

• work in an atmosphere free from oppressive behaviour, such as bullying, sexism and racism;

• reflect on what they do and understand its impact on others;

• respect other people's differences, particularly their feelings, values and beliefs;

• show initiative and are willing to take responsibility;

• have high levels of attendance and low levels of unauthorised absence.

INSPECTION FOCUS

This section is concerned with how well pupils respond to school in terms of their attitudes to learning, their behaviour, their values and personal development. The criteria cover pupils' responses to what the staff provide, through teaching and personal example, the curriculum, and the school's provision for spiritual, moral, social and cultural development.

Pupils' attitudes to learning and to other people depend upon the particular needs related to the pupils' disability or need. Their level of interest and response to school depends also on the competence of staff in employing specialist teaching skills to support approaches which engage the pupils actively and hold their interest in their learning. This sometimes requires pupils to overcome negative attitudes and behaviour.

In special schools and PRUs catering for pupils with emotional and behavioural difficulties, you must report behaviour as you find it, but take fully into account any improvements made since the pupils were admitted to the school or PRU. Pupils' levels and lengths of concentration and motivation may vary significantly across and within the age group in the foundation stage, each key stage and post-16. Observe their responses across the whole curriculum.

The personal development of pupils should be a high priority in special schools and PRUs. How well the pupils develop will reflect the extent to which they are independent and autonomous; feel personally fulfilled; achieve well and respond with optimism to challenges; develop social skills; and relate appropriately to peers and adults. The particular emphasis given will reflect pupils' special educational needs, their previous patterns of behaviour and attendance and their personal circumstances.

A particular focus of PRUs is to promote through the curriculum and the teaching the personal and social skills pupils need to return to their school, or transfer to college or work. Although pupils' behaviour and attendance may not yet be satisfactory all the time, you should pay particular attention to improvements pupils have made.

MAKING JUDGEMENTS

Make full use of the parents' meeting and discussions with pupils to gain their perspectives on what it is like to be a pupil in this school. If pupils enjoy coming to school, find out what it is about the provision that makes this so.

Use your evaluation of pupils' attitudes in lessons and your contacts with, and observations of, them at other times to decide how good attitudes and behaviour are in this school. You will need to find out the extent to which attitudes and behaviour help or hinder pupils' learning. In making your judgement about the values and personal development of the pupils, take into account your conclusions about how well the school provides opportunities for pupils' spiritual, moral, social and cultural development, and how the school helps pupils develop into responsible individuals, and relate well to each other.

The following characteristics illustrate where to pitch judgements about the attitudes, values and personal development of pupils, but will vary according to the type and needs of pupils.

Very good or excellent	Pupils are very positive about what the school has to offer and take a full part in the school's activities. They are keen to do well and respond to challenges in learning with confidence, optimism and responsibility. They are making significant steps in their learning towards being independent and autonomous, and where appropriate about returning to mainstream provision or transfer to college or work. They have respect for each other and show a mature and growing understanding of each other and of different view points. They behave well in different contexts and always relate constructively towards their peers and adults. The attendance figures of the school are at or above the national average. Punctuality is good. Exclusions are rare.
Satisfactory or better	Most pupils like school and take part in the school's activities. They are making satisfactory steps in their learning towards being independent and autonomous and where appropriate about returning to mainstream provision and transfer to college or work. Pupils are kind and considerate and show an increasing respect to each other and a willingness to listen. They behave appropriately in different contexts and generally relate constructively towards their peers and adults. They are punctual to lessons and rarely absent.

However, attitudes, values and personal development **cannot be satisfactory** if there are more than isolated instances of:

- taking little or no responsibility and initiative in their own learning;

- disruptive, aggressive or intimidating behaviour;

- racist attitudes or sexist language or behaviour;

- being managed through high levels of physical intervention by school staff.

Example 2.2.1

Extract from a report (SLD/PMLD)

Pupils have very good attitudes to their learning. Parents say their children love to come to school and miss it during holidays. When pupils arrive at school, they are happy and looking forward to their day. Despite their difficulties, they try very hard and work to the best of their ability. They are quick to celebrate their successes and those of others, and are willing to join in as fully as they can in all activities. They listen carefully to instructions, concentrate and persevere to complete tasks. Pupils with profound and multiple learning difficulties respond well to the stimulus of physical activities, such as swimming, and to tasks that form part of the sensory curriculum. These pupils are valued members of every class group and enjoy the friendship and help of their peer group.

[Overall: excellent attitudes (1)]

REPORTING REQUIREMENTS

SUMMARY REPORT	In both FULL and SHORT INSPECTIONS complete the table PUPILS' ATTITUDES, VALUES AND PERSONAL DEVELOPMENT. Write brief evaluations about the strengths and weaknesses under the table.
	If any of these are a feature of improvement of the school, record this in HOW THE SCHOOL HAS IMPROVED SINCE ITS LAST INSPECTION.
	Any aspects that are particularly good or need to improve should be reported under WHAT THE SCHOOL DOES WELL or WHAT COULD BE IMPROVED.
SHORT INSPECTIONS	If pupils' attitudes, values or personal development are either a strength of the school or a weakness they should become an issue in the commentary.
FULL INSPECTIONS	Report under the heading PUPILS' ATTITUDES, VALUES AND PERSONAL DEVELOPMENT.

GUIDANCE ON USING THE CRITERIA

☐ Pupils' attitudes to the school

Are pupils keen and eager to come to school? Do they show interest in school life and are they involved in the range of activities the school provides?

Notice how pupils greet staff at the start of the day, when many may have had long journeys. See if they move around the school calmly and with purpose. Are they pleased to show you around and point out their own work as well as that of others? Pupils who are interested and involved will be keen to work in lessons, answer questions, engage with the task in hand, participate in the range of activities provided and show enthusiasm to get as much out of school as possible.

When pupils' attitudes to the school are good, consider the reasons why. These may include:

- good teaching and interesting lessons;
- pupils being clear about the way they should behave;
- successful links between home and school;
- the school values the cultural traditions, aspirations and values pupils bring with them from home and their communities.

Consider the attitudes of different groups of pupils to the school and, where there are differences, find out why. See if the school is aware of them and find out what is being done, if anything, about them.

Example 2.2.2

Extract from a report

On many occasions pupils, frequently those in Year 10, are unwilling to begin work. They are uninterested in schoolwork, show little enthusiasm and many find it difficult to deal with getting things wrong. Often, with staff support and encouragement, they settle to what they have been asked to do and become involved in the activity. However, when pupils take too long to begin their work, as in an English lesson on myths and legends, or refuse to attempt work at all, as in a mathematics lesson on graphs, this clearly prevents them from making any real progress.

[Contributes to a judgement of poor attitudes (6)]

☐ Behaviour, including the incidence of exclusions

Do pupils behave well in lessons and around the school, are they courteous, trustworthy and respectful of the property of others?

Evaluate pupils' behaviour throughout the school day, in classrooms with teachers and when they are at break or lunch. Notice if pupils are polite to each other and to adults, and if they look after their own property as well as that of others. Take account of the views expressed by parents either at the parents' meeting and/or the questionnaires. Look at the behaviour policy in the school, and find out if pupils contributed to it or know about it. Independent schools are legally required to maintain incident and punishment books that should be scrutinised by the inspection team to assess whether any levels of misbehaviour observed are the norm or caused by additional visitors to the school. If an independent school does not have, or does not properly maintain, either an incident or punishment book, this failure should be a key issue.

In those schools and PRUs where pupils' behaviour is the main influence on their ability to learn and achieve well, you should take account of the time pupils have attended, their previous misbehaviour and personal circumstances. In these schools pupils' behaviour can change rapidly, often for reasons beyond the immediate control of the school. However, improvements in behaviour should be discernible in the majority of cases, when pupils have been attending the school or PRU for more than one term. Evidence includes pupils' records and the use of any profile on entry as a context for observations and assessment of behaviour during the inspection.

You should take account of the following in determining whether behaviour is as good as it reasonably could be:

■ whether the work in lessons and other opportunities are sufficiently challenging and engaging to reduce the incidence of inappropriate behaviour;

■ the school's or PRU's policies and procedures in promoting good behaviour are clear and consistently applied, and staff are skilled in dealing with difficult behaviour;

■ the extent to which pupils themselves are aware, or made aware of their own behaviour and its consequences, and have strategies to manage it more effectively.

You must report if the behaviour observed represents any danger to pupils or staff. If you judge the behaviour of pupils to be poor, you should indicate clearly whether the school or PRU through its organisation, policies and procedures has done as much as possible to minimise inappropriate behaviour.

In special schools you should consider the number of exclusions, the number of pupils involved, the reasons for the exclusions and the length of time out of school. You should consider how well the school reintegrates pupils after a period of exclusion.

In PRUs, you should consider the incidence of exclusions, including pupils who, though not formally excluded, are taken off the roll of the PRU on account of difficult behaviour or other management reasons and are provided with alternative provision under the LEA's policy of education other than at school.

☐ **Personal development and relationships**

Do pupils show initiative and are they willing to take responsibility?

Find out if, for example, pupils and students:

- take an active part in the day-to-day life and organisation of the school;

- show by their attitudes that they see themselves as part of the school community;

- support and care for each other;

- are able to play and organise their own work and study with minimal supervision;

- are more confident as they grow older.

At different times, pupils should be given some opportunity to be responsible for the younger children. This may involve working with them, for example, sharing a book, helping to tidy up different activities or caring for plants or pets.

Do pupils form constructive relationships with one another, and with teachers and other adults?

Most of the evidence about relationships and personal development will come from your observations of pupils around the school, and in other contexts such as work experience on link courses. For some pupils, improving how they relate to their peers and adults is fundamental to their chances of learning successfully and, where appropriate, returning to mainstream school, college, training or work. For pupils with complex learning disabilities, the quality of the relationships with staff is of vital importance. Observe how, through prolonged eye contact and body language, pupils demonstrate how well they relate to staff and how this provides a springboard for further learning. Look for evidence of pupils working and playing well together, particularly those from different minority ethnic backgrounds.

Do pupils reflect on and understand the impact of what they do on others? Do they respect the feelings, values and beliefs of others?

Observe the extent to which pupils are able to listen to what others have to say and respond positively to ideas, views and feelings different from their own. Evaluate how well the pupils have learned to respect differences and understand the feelings, values and beliefs of others.

Do pupils work in an atmosphere free from oppressive behaviour, such as bullying, sexism and racism?

Pupils can occasionally feel bullied or intimidated. Talk to pupils to find out if they know who to go to if they have a problem, how it is dealt with and whether they feel supported.

You need to assess how aware the adults in the school are and what steps they take to promote positive role models and counter negative attitudes throughout the school.

Evaluate the extent to which pupils are encouraged to work in mixed ethnic and gender groups.

☐ Attendance

Are there high levels of attendance?

Attendance in most special schools is usually good. You will not have a *PICSI report*, but you can compare the school's data to other similar special schools for reference using the data in the *PICSI* annex. However, you should base your judgements as in primary and secondary schools, if it is below 95 per cent or if you have concerns, for example about a downward trend.

In some special schools and PRUs, attendance will often be lower than 95 per cent because of pupils' previous educational history and personal circumstances. Some pupils may be dual registered. In these cases, you should calculate the number of sessions pupils attend as a proportion of the sessions expected at the special school or PRU. You should be aware that many of these pupils may be engaged in 'approved educational activities' which do not take place at the special school or PRU. These must be marked accordingly in the register and not as an authorised absence.

Whether attendance is lower than 95 per cent or not, the previous record of, for example, disaffected or school phobic pupils, should be examined so that **progress** can be fully evaluated. One or two pupils' records of attendance may well distort the overall figures. The key issue is whether improvement and attendance and punctuality has been achieved since pupils enrolled. You should examine registers and other information to gain a view about improvements in attendance over say a 6 or 12-month period. Look at the strategies the school uses in partnership with the educational welfare service to reduce the levels of unauthorised absence, and where it is an issue, truancy and absconding to a minimum.

You should consider the school's own analysis of attendance data, especially, if there are, for example, differences between boys and girls, year groups or pupils of minority ethnic background.

3. HOW WELL ARE PUPILS OR STUDENTS TAUGHT?

Inspectors must evaluate and report on:

☐ the quality of teaching, judged in terms of its impact on pupils' learning and what makes it successful or not.

Inspectors must include evaluations of:

- **how well the skills of literacy and numeracy are taught,** particularly to pupils of primary age and any pupils of secondary age whose reading, writing or numeracy is poor;

- **how well the teaching meets the needs of all its pupils,** taking account of their age, gender, ethnicity, capability, special educational needs, gifted and talented pupils, and those for whom English is an additional language;

- **the teaching in each subject,** commenting on any variations between subjects and year groups;

☐ how well pupils learn and make progress.

In determining their judgements, inspectors should consider the extent to which teachers:

- show good subject knowledge and understanding in the way they present and discuss their subject;

- are technically competent in teaching phonics and other basic skills;

- plan effectively, setting clear objectives that pupils understand;

- challenge and inspire pupils, expecting the most of them, so as to deepen their knowledge and understanding;

- use methods which enable all pupils to learn effectively;

- manage pupils well and insist on high standards of behaviour;

- use time, support staff and other resources, especially information and communications technology, effectively;

- assess pupils' work thoroughly and use assessments to help and encourage pupils to overcome difficulties;

- use homework effectively to reinforce and/or extend what is learned in school;

and the extent to which pupils:

- acquire new knowledge or skills, develop ideas and increase their understanding;

- apply intellectual, physical or creative effort in their work;

- are productive and work at a good pace;

- show interest in their work, are able to sustain concentration and think and learn for themselves;

- understand what they are doing, how well they have done and how they can improve.

INSPECTION FOCUS

Evaluation of the quality and impact of teaching is central to inspection. Teaching is fundamental to the quality of education provided by the school and is the main avenue through which the school contributes to pupils' attainment, progress and attitudes. The effectiveness of teaching and the consequent rate, breadth, depth and consolidation of pupils' learning are intrinsically connected. It is the skill of rigorous and perceptive inspection to find, illustrate and evaluate the links between the two.

When evaluating the quality of teaching and learning in the school, the process of education, you should concentrate on these priorities:

■ evaluating the quality of teaching, in terms of how effective it is;

■ identifying which aspects of teaching work best, or least well;

■ recording and reporting these insights so as to illustrate good practice and to explain weaknesses clearly so as to provide a basis for improvement.

In every lesson observed, you should consider:

■ the subject matter, its context and relevance, and how it relates to the pupils and what they have done before;

■ the methods used and structure of the lesson, evaluating each of the lesson's components where these are distinct (as in a 'literacy hour');

■ the pupils, what they are required to do and how they do it, noticing the extent to which the lesson is engaging or addressing the needs of all of them as fully as it should.

Often teachers and teaching or special support assistants work as a team. The latter make a valuable contribution to teaching and you should evaluate their contribution, providing feedback to support assistants in the way you do for teachers wherever possible. Final assessments of teaching, however, should only be provided for qualified teachers employed by the school. The work of teaching support staff however should feature in the teaching section of full reports.

TEACHING

Your insights stem from detailed classroom observation of teaching and pupils at work, complemented by the depth of understanding pupils show in discussion with you, where applicable, and your analysis of the quality and standards of the work they have done. This will enable you to see whether pupils are learning as rapidly and as well as you expect, and judge the quality of the teaching.

You need to explain your judgements by exemplifying what it is the teacher actually does that helps to make learning successful or not and you need to know what could be done to improve it further. You should not become side-tracked in the pursuit of individual criteria at the expense of missing the key points in a lesson.

Teachers in special schools and PRUs have the challenge of adapting and fashioning their teaching skills so as to enable pupils to learn effectively, in spite of their physical, sensory, emotional, behavioural or learning disabilities. The more successful the teaching, the less noticeable is the disability. You should attempt to capture the essence of this teaching so that it can best reflect the particular work of the school and the special needs of the pupils.

You should pay attention to how the skills of communication, numeracy, personal social and health education are taught and, especially in the case of PRUs, how the teaching increases (or otherwise) the prospect of pupils transferring back to mainstream school or to progress onto college, training or work.

For pupils of primary age, the teaching will focus mostly on the teacher responsible for the class who normally covers most or all of the curriculum. In schools for secondary aged pupils, there is likely to be more specialist teaching particularly at Key Stage 4 and post-16. In all special schools and PRUs, it is normal to find at least an equal number of learning support assistants who work together as a team and are involved together in the teaching. The work of learning support assistants therefore and its evaluation is an important part of your overall judgements.

Judging teaching in subjects

In SHORT INSPECTIONS, in special schools, judge the quality of teaching overall, based on the lessons seen, across subjects with an emphasis on observations of English and mathematics and personal, social and health education. You should make sure your judgements overall are based on evidence of teaching across the whole age range and subjects taught, and include all aspects of teaching relevant to the disabilities, including multi-sensory work and mobility.

On FULL INSPECTIONS, apart from PRUs, judgements about teaching in subjects are drawn from your *Evidence Forms* and recorded in the *Inspection Notebook*. Use the separate guidance on the inspection of subjects to identify the appropriate strengths and weaknesses in the subject at each Key Stage.

For both SHORT and FULL INSPECTIONS, you may evaluate the impact on pupils' progress of the work of therapists employed by health authorities, especially when staff at the school implement their programmes. You should not directly inspect them in individual lessons unless they are teaching groups supported by the teacher.

Judging the overall quality of teaching in the school

Teaching overall is likely to be unsatisfactory if more than approximately one in ten lessons are so judged. If these contain poor or very poor teaching, or the proportion is higher than one in eight, you will need to consider whether the school has serious weaknesses. Once the proportion of unsatisfactory teaching reaches one lesson in five it is very likely to be in need of special measures. If most of the teaching in the school is good, with much of it very good or better, and there is no unsatisfactory teaching, the overall quality of teaching could be judged very good because of the consistently good or very good teaching.

Reporting on teaching in the school needs to be crystal clear in terms of what works, what does not, why, and what should be done about it. Make sure there is consistency between the messages you give on how well pupils are taught and the other two major areas of inspection: standards and the leadership and management of the school. Excellent leadership and management, for example, do not sit comfortably with teaching which is simply satisfactory with a few good lessons.

Judging teaching in lessons

The following characteristics illustrate where to pitch judgements about how well pupils are taught in lessons.

Very good or excellent	The teaching of skills and subject matter is fully informed by a detailed understanding of the pupils' learning disabilities. Teaching is knowledgeable, stimulating and exciting, uses resources imaginatively, and makes intellectual and creative demands on pupils to be confident and effective learners. Good planning ensures that learning outcomes for individuals are clear and directly linked to challenging targets. Teachers relate to pupils in a way which is consistently encouraging and which promotes their confidence, achievement and self-sufficiency through constant feedback. Questioning and explaining are used well to consolidate, extend and verify what pupils know, understand and can do. The methods chosen are well matched to the pupils' needs and the demands of the curriculum, making the most productive use of other expertise and time available. Pupils' contributions are valued and respected. Pupils are keen to learn independently. They rise to challenges and try to think further for themselves. They work well for extended periods and, as a result, gains in knowledge and understanding, and engagement and participation in activities are very high.
Satisfactory or better	The teaching of communication skills and subject content is clear and accurate using explanation, demonstration and knowledge of the relevant learning disability to involve all pupils. The organisation of the lesson, planning and methods used, including questioning, allows most pupils to complete the work satisfactorily in the time available. Staff interact with pupils to check their understanding and to ensure they remain on task. The relationship between pupils and staff is such that they can work on their own confidently and they respond to feedback given positively.

However, teaching **cannot be satisfactory** if any one of the following is present:

- staff's knowledge of the areas of learning subjects, or pupils' disabilities is not good enough to promote demanding work;
- basic skills of communication are not taught effectively;
- a significant minority of pupils are not engaged in the lesson;
- lessons are poorly planned and organised and time is wasted;
- there are weaknesses in managing pupils' behaviour;
- pupils do not know, or are not sufficiently engaged to participate in, what they are doing;
- pupils are not making progress.

REPORTING REQUIREMENTS

SUMMARY REPORT	In both FULL and SHORT INSPECTIONS you must complete the table TEACHING AND LEARNING. In FULL INSPECTIONS, and where possible in SHORT INSPECTIONS, write brief comments about the quality of teaching in English and mathematics and personal, social and health education; strengths and weaknesses in teaching; how well the school meets the needs of all pupils; the percentages of satisfactory or better, very good or better and unsatisfactory or worse teaching; and particular strengths and weaknesses in pupils' learning.

If any of these are a feature of improvement in the school, report this in the section HOW THE SCHOOL HAS IMPROVED SINCE ITS LAST INSPECTION.

If any aspects of teaching are particularly good or need to improve you must report these under WHAT THE SCHOOL DOES WELL or WHAT COULD BE IMPROVED. |
| SHORT INSPECTIONS | In the commentary, expand your judgements on teaching as reported in either WHAT THE SCHOOL DOES WELL or WHAT COULD BE IMPROVED. Complete the data tables in Part C of the report, including the data on teaching. |
| FULL INSPECTIONS | Report fully under the heading HOW WELL ARE PUPILS TAUGHT? Complete the data tables in Part C of the report, including the data on teaching. |

Example 3.1

Extract from a report on a school for PMLD children

Teaching in the nursery is excellent. Creative, imaginative, innovative methodology is a strong feature. Learning is exciting and fun. Children spend their day responding to a rich and exciting curriculum where well-established routines give them security yet are enlivened with new stimuli. Children are constantly praised and encouraged throughout the day. The very effective teaching is carefully planned; learning objectives are clearly set out, and a range of inspirational and compelling resources is used as objects of reference which engross the children. Behaviour management is excellent and teachers show a sensitive regard for children's individual needs and care. Total communication strategies are consistently used alongside song and rhyme, and teachers have an acute awareness of each child's developing language patterns, skilfully responding to them to ensure repetition and consistency of response. These teachers know their children very well and show tremendous enthusiasm and commitment, which strongly promotes learning.

[An example of excellent teaching (1)]

In order to stress the importance of evaluating teaching through its impact, this guidance puts learning first. The criteria for learning are encapsulated in the questions: are the pupils engaged? challenged? extended? For teaching, the questions include: are pupils taught the right things in an effective manner and at the right pace?

☐ How well pupils learn and make progress

Do pupils acquire new knowledge or skills, develop ideas and increase their understanding?

In forming your judgements about the acquisition of knowledge, skills or understanding, take every opportunity to relate this to the work done previously. Learning may be consolidated or may cover new ground in the lesson you observe. Your judgements should, where possible, be referenced to what has gone before. The learning objectives identified by the teacher will help you to ask pupils relevant questions and to judge whether the teaching and learning are well matched to the pupils' age and capability. Whenever you can, record specific examples of how the teaching helps the pupils to understand more.

Examination of work and discussion with pupils will also help you to decide if the work in hand is building on pupils' current knowledge, understanding or skills. When you analyse samples of work, focus on evidence of progress over a period of time, and within year groups. Look for consistency of approach and content between classes covering the same age range. The analysis of work recorded on *Evidence Forms*, should provide detailed information about the rate, quantity and quality of pupils' learning, not simply a list of the content covered over time.

Discussion with pupils, where appropriate, about what they are doing can give you an insight into how they acquire new knowledge and skills, and increase their understanding across the subjects of the curriculum. On SHORT INSPECTIONS, this may be your prime source of evidence of work in some subjects.

Do pupils apply intellectual, physical or creative effort in their work and are they working productively and at a good pace?

Most pupils will make an effort in their work if the teaching makes demands and provides the encouragement which enables them to do so. You need to judge, therefore, the extent to which pupils are engaged in their work, whether the effort involved is enough, or too much, and whether it was worthwhile in relation to what has been learnt. In special schools and PRUs, the particular kind of effort, whether intellectual or creative, they need to make to accomplish tasks may well be considerable and should be recognised. Every lesson should contribute in some way towards the pupils' development or consolidation of knowledge, skills or understanding. Most pupils should be able to explain what they have done and what they have learnt at the end of each session. Pupils are far more likely to apply effort in their work when they see why they are working in a particular way, and what they are required to understand is important.

The amount of work pupils do, the extent to which they have to concentrate and their attitude to the tasks, will indicate if they are working to capacity. Pupils do not always work at a good pace unless the teacher expects them to. During lesson observations try to return to the same pupils more than once to judge if they are working well enough and getting through the required amount of work. This also provides evidence of the teacher's use of time and understanding of pupils' learning disabilities. Good teaching routines encourage pupils to manage their own time well and to get through what is required in the time available.

Do pupils show interest in their work? Are they able to sustain concentration and thinking and learn for themselves? Do pupils understand what they are doing, how well they have done and how they can improve?

Pupils are likely to show interest and understanding when the tasks, activities and challenges presented are lively and interesting. Effective teachers constantly relate new learning to old, encouraging pupils to make the links between areas of learning and to think imaginatively for themselves.

These aspects of learning are especially important in special schools and PRUs because pupils often need considerable help to engage with tasks, to sustain concentration and work independently. Consider the extent to which pupils show interest and curiosity, and how they tackle tasks. Observe how well they concentrate over periods of time, appropriate to their abilities; how well pupils listen to staff and their peers, draw on their own ideas and use them productively; how active they are in taking responsibility for their own learning; how well they think independently and find things out for themselves. You should find out the extent to which pupils are aware of what they are doing and understand what they have done, and are able to make use of feedback from staff and peers to help them improve.

☐ **The quality of teaching, judged in terms of its impact on pupils' learning and what makes it successful or not**

Do teachers show good subject knowledge and understanding in the way they present and discuss their subject?

Evaluate the success of teaching and what makes it so. For teachers of young children, who have not yet embarked on the National Curriculum programmes of study, their subject knowledge is what they know and understand about the content of the Early Learning Goals and of how children develop. You can judge teachers' subject knowledge by observing, for example:

■ how competently they teach the content of the Early Learning Goals, National Curriculum programmes of study and the RE syllabus;

■ how competently they plan the area of work and learning in the subject or show a good understanding of the way the subject develops;

■ how well they teach the skills of communication (including literacy) and numeracy;

■ their skills in asking subject specific questions which help pupils to understand and which extend their thinking;

■ how well they explain new ideas in a way that make sense to pupils;

■ how well they draw on their knowledge of how children learn, and the implications for learning of their disabilities when presenting them with new experiences or information;

■ how well they use equipment, artefacts and resources to interest and challenge the pupils;

■ their ability to deepen the thinking in the subject for all pupils and stretch the more able.

Are teachers technically competent in teaching phonics and other basic skills?

TEACHING LITERACY

The National Literacy Strategy, including the literacy hour, is non-statutory and special schools and PRUs may have alternative approaches designed to improve standards in communication including reading and writing. You must form a view about the impact of the school's strategies on the quality of teaching and the standards achieved.

Very good teachers of literacy skills combine competence in the full range of technical knowledge with the flair to put it across in ways which make language come alive for children. **Where it is appropriate** you should be looking for:

- thorough knowledge of the National Literacy Strategy (NLS) Framework for teaching;

- secure knowledge and understanding of the literacy knowledge and skills to be taught;

- secure knowledge and understanding of the literacy skills which pupils need;

- a good understanding of how to teach phonics including phonological awareness, the blending of sounds in words for reading, segmenting words into sounds for spelling, and a knowledge of spelling rules;

- good use of the NLS teaching objectives in short- and medium-term planning;

- the right balance between word, sentence and text level work.

Teaching numeracy within the dedicated mathematics lesson

The *National Numeracy Strategy: Framework for Teaching Mathematics* has been introduced for all schools, and complements the National Literacy Strategy. You must form a view about the impact of the school's strategy for numeracy on the quality of teaching and the standards achieved. When completing *Evidence Forms* evaluate each component of the daily lesson for mathematics.

Where special schools and PRUs are making use of the *National Numeracy Strategy: Framework for Teaching Mathematics* you should be looking at:

- the quality of teachers' plans – whether the school makes good use of the objectives listed in the Framework to establish progression in pupils' learning;

- the extent to which pupils are informed about the learning objectives, the mathematical skills and knowledge they are to learn, what they are to do, how long it should take and the progress they are making;

- how effectively the teacher's introduction to the mathematics lesson engages all pupils, sets a brisk pace, and encourages and enables pupils to participate in oral and mental work, by giving pupils appropriate thinking time, promoting quick recall skills and efficient mental calculation strategies;

- the teacher's and pupils' correct use of mathematical vocabulary and notation providing the language for pupils to explain their thinking, solutions and strategies, and helping pupils to interpret and make accurate use of words and symbols;

- how well the teacher explains, demonstrates and illustrates the mathematics being taught – drawing on the class for ideas, solutions, methods and practical contributions; uses well-focused questions that provide opportunities to check pupils' understanding and to correct any mistakes; and employs resources to establish mathematical relationships or properties, and to assist in communication with the pupils;

■ whether the activities pupils are engaged in are appropriately matched to the intended learning objectives and are suitably adapted to meet the learning needs of pupils within different ability groups;

■ how effectively the lesson is concluded, whether the teacher highlights: the key facts, ideas and vocabulary pupils have learned and need to remember; identifies what has been achieved; looks forward to the next lesson; and sets any out-of-class work or homework to consolidate or extend the mathematics in the lesson;

■ teachers' knowledge of mathematics and of the mathematics curriculum – whether teachers make appropriate use of the Framework's objectives and examples to help to identify progression over time and the methods of calculation that pupils are to be taught, are quick to recognise pupils' mistakes and use these as teaching points, and can identify key ideas in mathematics and relationships between topics.

Do teachers plan effectively, setting clear objectives that pupils understand?

In a lesson, session or sequence of lessons, look for clear objectives for what pupils are to learn, which are directly linked to their targets in IEPs. In special schools and PRUs, lesson planning will necessarily involve choosing subject content to be taught in ways that enable different needs to be met. You will need to judge whether the planning is successful in achieving the targets set for pupils. Check that pupils understand the purpose of the task so that they can make choices and work independently.

During the inspection, you should discuss with teachers how lessons link in the long term with pupils' IEPs. Consider how effectively support staff are involved in lesson planning and in the teaching to help pupils learn and achieve their targets, and how they are briefed about what they are expected to do.

Example 3.2

Extract from a report on teaching (PMLD)

Lessons are very well planned, following the very good quality schemes of work and support material provided by subject co-ordinators. Teachers are usually quite clear about what it is they want the pupils to learn. Lessons are frequently very carefully structured, so that the pace of pupils' learning is controlled, and their interest is sustained. For example, music lessons often contain an effective sequence of calm and exciting activities, and of sound and silence. In some lessons, teachers work together, and their joint planning is usually most effective. This is particularly striking when it involves teachers from other schools, as in an excellent dance performance, involving Key Stage 3 and 4 pupils with profound and multiple learning difficulties. In lessons where pupils of differing attainment are taught together, teachers plan carefully to give access to the curriculum to pupils with additional difficulties; for example, preparing extra lesson materials which pupils can feel or smell or ensuring that pupils are 'danced' in wheelchairs or in the arms of staff so that they experience as fully as possible what other pupils are able to do without help.

[Contributes to a judgement of very good teaching (2)]

Do teachers challenge and inspire pupils, expecting the most of them, so as to deepen their knowledge and understanding?

Evaluate the extent to which teachers challenge pupils to imaginative and intellectual effort. To what extent do they provide pupils with surprising and exciting opportunities that extend their knowledge? Teaching that is inspiring is seen in pupils' sustained concentration and reflection, the reshaping of their ideas, or in original and imaginative work.

Do teachers use methods which enable all pupils to learn effectively?

Consider how well teachers match the methods they use to the purpose of the lesson and to the needs of pupils. The key to the judgements you make is whether these methods and their organisation are likely to result in high standards of work and behaviour for all pupils. If there are any pupils, or groups of pupils, who are not involved and not learning effectively, then you must find out the reasons for this. Consider specifically whether the methods used support the diverse range of pupils' need, and, where relevant, those pupils for whom English is an additional language.

You will need to evaluate whether:

- the teacher's exposition or explanation is lively, informative and well structured;

- any grouping by ability promotes higher standards;

- the teacher's use and style of questioning probes pupils' knowledge and understanding, challenges their thinking and engages all pupils;

- practical activity is purposeful and not stereotyped in that pupils are encouraged to think about what they are doing, what they have learned from it and how to improve their work;

- investigations and problem-solving activities help pupils to apply and extend their learning in new contexts;

- the choice of pupil grouping, for example pupils working alone, in pairs or small groups or all together, achieves the objectives for teaching and learning;

- the form of organisation allows the teacher to interact efficiently with as many pupils as possible;

- the use of resources stimulates learning and sensitively reflects different groups, culture and backgrounds;

- learning targets are set and, where appropriate, negotiated with pupils individually or within a group;

- work is planned effectively so that all staff can work flexibly, responding to individual needs as they arise.

Example 3.3

Extract from a report on a PRU (primary age)

An English lesson with one class showed many of the characteristics of the best teaching at the unit. The aims and learning objectives for the lesson were linked clearly to a previous mathematics lesson about pyramids. The pupils looked up spellings in a dictionary, then used the definitions in other activities. The whole lesson fitted into the class topic about Egyptians. The activities were explained enthusiastically at the beginning of the session. The relationships between staff and pupils were very good indeed, which supported the pupils' learning. The teacher had absolutely secure knowledge of the subject matter and explained things patiently and clearly. As pupils began to succeed, the teacher praised them enthusiastically, which made the pupils proud of their achievements. The tuition assistant made a significant and positive contribution to the quality of pupils' learning by supporting them, but allowing them to develop their independent skills. The teamwork between adults was excellent. Management of the pupils was consistent and unobtrusive, which minimised any disruption caused by occasional silly behaviour.

[Contributes to a judgement of very good teaching (2)]

Do teachers manage pupils well and insist on high standards of behaviour?

Your judgements here will need to take full account of the particular kind of challenge posed by the pupils to staff. For some pupils, ensuring that behaviour is good is the most important issue because of their previous educational histories. How staff anticipate and intervene to encourage good behaviour and avoid conflict is central to their teaching skills and underpinned by the quality of their relationships with pupils. Observe how staff by their careful planning, use of consistent approaches, teamwork and a well-judged combination of challenge and encouragement, minimise inappropriate behaviour and help pupils to learn more effectively. Sometimes, despite the efforts of staff, pupils' behaviour may be unsatisfactory or poor. In these circumstances you should judge whether staff deal with difficult incidents well.

Do teachers use time, support staff and other resources, especially information and communications technology (ICT), effectively?

For all pupils, in both special schools and PRUs, a key teaching skill is how effectively time, resources – including support staff – and ICT are used. Observe whether staff inject pace into lessons by the use of a wide range of techniques to ensure that pupils remain on task, such as regular prompting about what they are doing, reminders about how long they have to complete tasks, and by the use of a wide range of learning materials to teach a particular skill where practice and reinforcement for learning is necessary. Invariably, the success of the teaching is dependent on the quality of teamwork between teachers and support assistants. Judge the clarity of roles, the flexibility of all staff to do whatever is necessary and how this teamwork enables pupils to learn more effectively and gain in independence.

As you evaluate the work of teachers in teaching information and communications technology, check to see that it centres upon the teachers' expectation of pupils in their use of resources and their development or consolidation of knowledge. You need to observe the pupils and the teachers' interaction with them to find out if there is a clearly understood expectation of what the pupils should be doing and why. The activity may be planned to develop IT capability, support learning within the subject, or both. For some pupils, the effective use of ICT is critical in enabling pupils to participate fully in the learning and achieve maximum independence. How effectively teachers use ICT is dependent upon the clarity of their intention and the quality of intervention and support given during the use of ICT. You need to judge whether the intervention by the teacher merely solves technical problems or maintains pupils' attention upon the task. Does it enhance pupils' understanding of ICT, the subject or both? When parents or support staff are directed by the teacher to help pupils using ICT, they too need to be aware of what the teacher expects from the use of the ICT and what they should do to ensure the intended learning takes place.

Do teachers assess pupils' work thoroughly and use assessments to help and encourage pupils to overcome difficulties?

Your judgements about teachers' assessment of their pupils should focus on how well teachers look for gains in learning, gaps in knowledge and areas of misunderstanding, through their day-to-day work with pupils. This will include marking, questioning of individuals and plenary sessions. Clues to the effectiveness of formative assessment are how well the teachers listen and respond to pupils, encourage, and, where appropriate, praise them, recognise and handle misconceptions, build on their responses and steer them towards clearer understanding. Effective teachers encourage pupils to judge the success of their own work and set targets for improvement. They will take full account of the targets set out in pupils' individual education plans.

Do teachers use homework effectively to reinforce and/or extend what is learned in school?

When judging how well teachers make use of homework find out the school's policy and whether homework:

- is planned to integrate with classwork;

- is tailored to individual learning needs;

- helps pupils to learn independently;

- is regularly and constructively marked.

You should also establish whether parents understand how to help pupils with their homework.

How well does the teaching meet the needs of all pupils?

In this *Handbook* references have been made to the importance of evaluating the effectiveness of teaching and learning for all pupils. As an inspector, your thinking about the needs of all pupils and ensuring equal opportunities is not an optional extra but an integral aspect of all the judgements you make about teaching, as it is for the other sections of the inspection schedule.

In coming to judgements about how well teachers promote and provide for equal opportunities, you will need to assess whether or not the teaching methods, the access to resources and the time of day or year disadvantage any groups of pupils, for example if pupils were absent from school to celebrate Eid. You will also need to take account of pupils' ages, gender, ethnicity and capability on reaching your conclusions. For example, the choice of texts for the literacy hour might favour girls; pupils may be regularly withdrawn from mathematics in order to practise reading skills or for instrumental music tuition; the religious background of the pupils prevents them from taking part in activities which promote their spiritual or cultural development; or, unavoidable lateness to school may result in a pupil always missing the introduction to work in science.

Pay particular attention to the school's provision for three identified groups of pupils: those with special educational needs; those who have English as an additional language; and gifted and talented pupils.

How well does the school meet the needs of pupils with special educational needs?

When judging how well the teaching meets the needs of pupils with special educational needs in PRUs, look for the impact on the learning of pupils on the register of SEN. The teacher's plans should ensure that the work is matched to pupils' needs and show how the pupils are making progress. The effectiveness of planning is important because it enables the SEN coordinator, or LEA SEN support staff to liaise successfully with teachers, whether the pupils are supported in class or are withdrawn from lessons. Check to see that IEPs contain clear targets and are sufficiently practical for class teachers to implement when support staff are not present.

In special schools, your judgements should apply to those pupils with additional physical, sensory, emotional or learning difficulties from the majority of pupils in the school, and for whom there is a need to provide further modifications to the teaching programmes.

Example 3.4

Extract from a report

Staff have comprehensive knowledge of the range of special educational needs within their group, in particular the educational implications of autism. They have strong relationships with external professionals, including educational psychologists, health visitors and speech therapists, working in partnership to provide the children with appropriate educational provision. These relationships, together with the high level of knowledge staff have about managing specific programmes in group activities, ensure that teaching meets the needs of all children most of the time.

How well does the school meet the needs of pupils with English as an additional language?

You should evaluate whether the planning and teaching methods take account of the language and learning needs of pupils with English as an additional language (EAL). This involves the identification of those who need additional support; not just when they are in the early stages of learning English, but also those at more advanced levels whose literacy skills often fail to do justice to their academic potential. Giving appropriate support will consist of some or all of the following:

- ensuring pupils have opportunities for supported speaking and listening;

- providing effective models of spoken and written language (for example, through writing frames);

- understanding how the first language can be used to support the learning of the second;

- using high-quality, culturally relevant visual aids and other resources;

- providing bilingual support assistants.

In inspecting EAL, you should look to see whether all the work is firmly placed within the National Curriculum. Withdrawal of pupils from lessons should be kept to a minimum, and their teaching needs to contain the same features as those outlined above.

4. HOW GOOD ARE THE CURRICULAR AND OTHER OPPORTUNITIES OFFERED TO PUPILS OR STUDENTS?

Inspectors must evaluate and report on:

☐ the quality and range of opportunities for learning provided by the school for all pupils, highlighting features which are particular strengths and weaknesses in the foundation subjects, Key Stages and post-16;

including specific comment on:

- **extra-curricular activities** including study support;
- **the provision made for personal, social and health education,** including sex education and attention to drug misuse;
- **work related education,** including careers education and guidance for secondary-age pupils;
- **the quality of links with the community and with other schools or colleges;**

☐ whether the school meets statutory curricular requirements, including provision of religious education where appropriate;

☐ how well the school cultivates pupils' personal – including spiritual, moral, social and cultural – development.

In determining their judgements, inspectors should consider the extent to which the school:

- provides a broad range of worthwhile opportunities which meet the interests, aptitudes and particular needs of pupils;
- has effective strategies for teaching the basic skills of literacy and numeracy;
- provides enrichment through its extra-curricular provision including support for learning outside the school day;
- is socially inclusive by ensuring equality of access and opportunity for all pupils;
- provides pupils with the knowledge and insights into values and beliefs and enables them to reflect on their experiences in a way which develops their spiritual awareness and self-knowledge;
- promotes principles which distinguish right from wrong;
- encourages pupils to take responsibility, show initiative and develop an understanding of living in a community;
- teaches pupils to appreciate their own cultural traditions and the diversity and richness of other cultures;
- provides effectively for personal and social education, including health education, sex education and attention to drug misuse;
- provides, for secondary-age pupils, effective careers education and guidance, work experience, and vocational education;
- has links with the community which contribute to pupils' learning;
- has constructive relationships with partner institutions such as link schools.

INSPECTION FOCUS

Your inspection should centre on the extent to which the content and organisation of the curriculum provide access to the full range of learning experiences and promote the attainment, progress and personal development of all pupils. The curriculum comprises all the planned activities within and beyond the timetabled day.

All special schools (including hospital schools) and PRUs must provide pupils with a broad, balanced and relevant curriculum which when taught enables them to make progress in relation to their priority needs.

PRUs and hospital special schools are not obliged by statute to teach the programmes of study of the National Curriculum, or religious education, although many will plan from them.

Pupils in PRUs should have a 'full-time' curriculum, possibly made up by individually arranged packages, according to age and need. All pupils should have a curriculum that includes English and mathematics (and science at Key Stages 1–3), and creative activities such as art and drama, design and technology and physical education. The curriculum should comply with the LEA curriculum policy for all PRUs and reflect the LEA's policy on the curriculum of pupils who receive education otherwise than at school.

Special schools serving pupils of primary age, have flexibility in the way they cover the programmes of study for art, design and technology, geography, history, music and physical education, whilst maintaining a balanced and broadly based curriculum which must include the six non-core subjects.

Special schools must implement the programmes of study of the National Curriculum unless modifications or disapplications are made, either for individual pupils through their statement or, at Key Stage 4, by dropping specific subjects using the permitted flexibility. The position for pupils under 5 or in reception is that, the curriculum should be based on the Early Learning Goals. For students aged 16–19, the curriculum should be distinctive, reflecting the need to provide a range of options suitable for students as they are about to leave school and move on to further education, training or work, in accordance with their needs.

In those special schools which serve pupils who make very small steps in progress, compared to their peers, you should ascertain how the school makes use of the facility to use the programmes of study flexibly, so that pupils have their entitlement to a broad and balanced curriculum, in age-appropriate but challenging contexts. These schools will need to keep up to date with any new requirements arising from the review of the National Curriculum, as it applies to pupils working towards level 1 in all subjects, and at each stage.

Effective schools help pupils to become confident people with enduring values, able to contribute effectively to society in accordance with their ability to do so. The experiences offered are rich and stimulating, contributing to the personal development of all individuals and so help them prepare for life as adults by being as independent as possible.

In your assessment of the opportunities offered to pupils you should find out what the school is really good at. Take note of any areas of excellence. The good school will ensure that the quality and range of opportunities for learning covers all the key aspects of personal development, with the emphasis on the whole child and all-round development, and the provision for **spiritual, moral, social and cultural development.**

MAKING JUDGEMENTS

A wide range of evidence contributes to the evaluation of the curriculum. Before the inspection refer to *Forms S2* and *S3* to gauge the school's perception of how far it meets the statutory curriculum requirements and the DfEE recommendations for 'taught time' for each Key Stage. If the taught time falls below the recommended minimum, you must report this. Form an impression of the quality of what the school offers through your reading of the prospectus and other documents. This impression will be reinforced or rejected once you begin gathering evidence in the school.

In SHORT INSPECTIONS, extensive evaluation of curriculum provision is neither possible nor desirable, but must include whether or not it meets statutory requirements and how well it provides for the spiritual, moral, social and cultural development of pupils.

The following characteristics illustrate where to pitch judgements about the quality of the curriculum for a **PRU**.

Very good or excellent	The curriculum interprets the statutory requirements in stimulating, as well as structured, ways, and fully complies with the LEA's curriculum policy for PRUs. Very good attention is given to the core subjects. The curriculum provides good opportunities for pupils to gain accreditation for their achievements. It uses resources from within and outside the PRU very effectively to enrich the curriculum. High priority is given to pupils' personal development through opportunities for pupils to take responsibility, show initiative, become aware of their part in the wider community, and transfer successfully to mainstream school, college, training or work. Pupils understand what is right and wrong and respect the differences and similarities between people, their values and beliefs drawing on pupils' own cultural, religious and family beliefs.

Satisfactory or better	The curriculum meets the statutory requirements for providing a broadly based and balanced curriculum which complies with the LEA's curriculum policy for PRUs. There is an emphasis on the core subjects. Reasonable opportunities are provided for all pupils to gain accreditation for their achievements. Satisfactory attention is given to pupils' personal development to encourage them to take responsibility, to be aware of their part in the wider community and to transfer back to mainstream school, college, training or work. Reasonable use is made of resources within the community; visits and other activities are planned to contribute to pupils' learning. Pupils understand the difference between right and wrong, and respect the tradition, values and beliefs of others.

However, the curriculum **cannot be satisfactory** if:

- statutory requirements, including any significant aspects of the core subjects, are not met;

- it does not comply with the LEA's curriculum policy in relation to PRUs by omitting areas of work;

- it fails to provide an adequate programme of personal, social and health education, in line with the policy of the PRU;

- opportunities for promoting essential basic skills are neglected;

- it does little to inculcate respect, tolerance and good behaviour;

- it is unduly narrow in the opportunities for personal development or curriculum enrichment.

The following characteristics illustrate where to pitch judgements about the quality of the curriculum in a **special school**.

Very good or excellent	The curriculum at all stages interprets requirements in a stimulating, as well as structured ways; it provides good opportunities for the pupils to learn to communicate as effectively as they can. At Key Stages 3 and 4 it builds on the curriculum at Key Stages 1 and 2 and provides opportunities in an age-appropriate environment for pupils to communicate, become more independent and to gain in knowledge, skills and understanding. For students post-16, the curriculum provides a broad and balance range of opportunities for students to build on their skills of communication and to gain in independence, working where possible off-site, gaining the maximum external accreditation for their achievements. It uses resources from within and outside the school very effectively to enrich the curriculum. High priority is given to pupils' personal development through opportunities for pupils to take responsibility, initiative and become aware of their part in the school and wider community, and transfer successfully to mainstream school, college, training or work. Pupils understand what is right and wrong, and respect the differences and similarities between pupils, their values and beliefs, drawing on pupils' own cultural, religious and family beliefs.
Satisfactory or better	The curriculum meets statutory requirements for all Key Stages and provides satisfactory opportunities for pupils to become increasingly independent and to learn to communicate effectively. At later Key Stages, further opportunities are provided in an age-appropriate environment for pupils to gain in independence and have their achievement externally accredited. Reasonable use is made of resources within the community; visits and other activities are planned to contribute to pupils' learning. Some opportunities for responsibility are provided. Pupils are helped to understand the difference between right and wrong, and respect the traditions, values and beliefs of others.

However, the curriculum **cannot be satisfactory** if:

- statutory requirements, including any significant aspects of the core subjects at Key Stages 1 to 3 or in relation to pupils' statements, are not met;

- takes insufficient account of National Strategies for literacy and numeracy;

- it does little to inculcate respect, tolerance and good behaviour;

- it is unduly narrow in opportunities for personal development or curricular enrichment.

In SHORT INSPECTIONS, evaluation of curriculum provision must include whether or not it meets statutory requirements and how well it provides for the spiritual, moral, social and cultural development of pupils.

REPORTING REQUIREMENTS

SUMMARY REPORT	In all inspections, the first boxes of the table headed OTHER ASPECTS OF THE SCHOOL must be completed, with comment on particular strengths and weaknesses, and any areas that do not meet statutory requirements.
	If any of these are a feature of improvement in the school, record this in the section HOW THE SCHOOL HAS IMPROVED SINCE ITS LAST INSPECTION.
	Any aspects that are particularly good or need to improve should be reported under WHAT THE SCHOOL DOES WELL and WHAT COULD BE IMPROVED.
SHORT INSPECTIONS	Expand in the commentary WHAT THE SCHOOL DOES WELL or WHAT COULD BE IMPROVED.
FULL INSPECTIONS	Report under the heading HOW GOOD ARE THE CURRICULAR AND OTHER OPPORTUNITIES OFFERED TO PUPILS?

Example 4.1

Extract from a report (primary PRU)

The curriculum is sound at both Key Stages. Although the unit is not required to cover the National Curriculum, it provides a broad and balanced spread of subjects which relate closely to current requirements. This prepares pupils suitably for re-entry to school at an appropriate level. Effective literacy and numeracy policies and schemes of work are in place. These are securely based and work well, being written after wide consultation. Policies and schemes of work in other subjects are still evolving. As a result, there are some weaknesses in the arrangements for planning and monitoring continuity in pupils' learning.

[Overall: satisfactory curriculum (4)]

GUIDANCE ON USING THE CRITERIA

☐ The quality and range of opportunities for learning provided by the school for all pupils, including extra-curricular activities

☐ Whether the school meets statutory requirements, including provision of religious education where appropriate

Does the school provide a broad range of worthwhile opportunities which meet the interests, aptitudes and special needs of pupils?

Before the inspection you should refer to section D2 of *Form S2* to evaluate how the school allocates the time available to the different subjects of the curriculum. Your evaluation of the breadth and quality of the provision will require you to consider how the school has made decisions about what will be included in the curriculum, and the time allocated to different aspects, taking account of:

■ the programmes of study of the National Curriculum and the Early Learning Goals;

■ the importance of communication, especially literacy, and numeracy;

■ the current guidance from the Qualifications and Curriculum Authority (QCA);

■ the needs of all pupils and the curricular provision set out in statements;

■ the best use of the specialist skills of staff;

■ the organisation of the school day;

■ how the school ensures the needs of all pupils are met and that they have equal access to all areas of the curriculum and opportunities to succeed in them;

■ special programmes offered to pupils such as hydro and physiotherapy, mobility training and speech therapy;

■ the LEA's curricular policy for PRUs and the PRU curriculum statement.

In PRUs, you should find out from *Form S1* the number of pupils on the register of SEN, and what range of needs are represented. Find out how pupils with SEN are organised, for example in withdrawal groups, in-class support or setting, as the arrangements may make a difference to the curriculum pupils receive. Judge how well the curriculum is organised so as to meet the needs of pupils with SEN (or additional SEN in special schools), taking particular note of the provision as this forms the basis for further interventions by the school or from outside the school. Check that the arrangements for using IEPs are effective in ensuring that individual needs are addressed while enabling pupils to have full access to the curriculum.

Example 4.2

> ### Extract from a report (PMLD)
>
> *Excellent use is made of the sensory room and sensory resources, which create a stimulating atmosphere for children to learn through a wide range of experiences. Positioning of children with complex needs is very good. Excellent opportunities are provided through music and drama for children and adults to take part in intensive interaction which encourages a range of skills in communication. Dramatic involvement is built up over a series of lessons, which culminate in a 'performance'. Most of all, the lessons are fun, and the teachers and support staff and children clearly enjoy this work. Children respond unusually well to this work.*
>
> [Contributes to a judgement of a very good curriculum (2)]

Does the school have effective strategies for teaching the basic skills of literacy and numeracy?

Every school is required to have a strategy for teaching literacy and numeracy. Most schools reflect the National Literacy Strategy and the National Numeracy Strategy. Whether or not they do, you need to evaluate how effective their strategies are. In reaching this judgement you must take account of the results the school achieves in National Curriculum tests and any other assessments.

Does the school provide enrichment through its extra-curricular provision, including support for learning outside the school day?

The effective school seeks to help all pupils take advantage of opportunities to learn, for example visits out of school, running after-school homework clubs and extra-curricular activities at different times of the day so that all pupils who wish to can attend. The range of extra-curricular opportunities often depends on the skills and availability of staff and parents, but usually encompasses, at least, some sort of sport and musical activity. The opportunity to take part and the number of pupils involved in all such activities will contribute to your evaluation. In some special schools and PRUs provision may need to be limited to lunch times because of the distance pupils live from school.

Is the curriculum socially inclusive by ensuring equality of access and opportunity for all pupils?

You need to make sure that you have accurately defined groups of pupils who form the intake of the school which you will state in THE CHARACTERISTICS OF THE SCHOOL. Once you have defined the groups, check if your preliminary analysis of performance from the records indicates that there are any significant differences in the attainment, experience and benefit gained from what the school provides. If so use these to guide your observations, work sampling and discussions with pupils. Evaluate the extent to which:

- all pupils benefit according to need from what the school provides;

- any groups of pupils do not do as well as others and if the school is aware of this;

- the school offers justifiable explanations for any differences;

- the school has taken any effective action if needed.

- ☐ **For FULL INSPECTIONS only, the school's provision for personal, social and health education, and the quality of the school's links with the community and other schools, colleges and initial teacher training consortia**

Does the school provide for personal and social education, including health education, sex education and attention to drug misuse?

A crucial part of the whole curriculum is what is provided for personal, social and health education – note that drug misuse is a required topic to be covered by approved independent schools. The programme should be tailored to the particular needs of the pupils at the special school or PRU. Evaluate how successfully the school builds into pertinent activities such as mobility training, feeding programmes, the acquisition of personal skills, such as relating to and working with others, or coping with stress. In some cases it may be appropriate for a particular emphasis to be placed for a period of time on some aspect of the programme to deal with a pupil's pressing need.

You should establish whether provision is coherent, and appropriate to the ages and needs of pupils and judge whether pupils have a sound knowledge and understanding of health issues, and an awareness of their ability to make choices relating to their health. Sex education may be an element of health education provision if the appropriate authority have decided to include it as part of the curriculum.

Schools should decide how best to organise drug education for their pupils. They may provide it within science lessons, as appropriate within other subject areas, or as part of a broader programme of personal, social and health education. The essential aim of drug education should be to give pupils the facts, emphasise the benefits of a healthy lifestyle, and give children the knowledge and skills to make informed and healthy choices now and later in life.

Example 4.3

Extract from a report (PRU)

Personal and social education are well taught. Teachers have high expectations of pupils and present interesting, stimulating lessons which are relevant to pupils' personal needs – for example, in fostering co-operation and developing self-esteem. Topics are challenging and a good pace is maintained in lessons. All written work is marked, with useful, supportive comments. Pupils' obvious enthusiasm for this subject reflects the strength of its teaching, seen for example in a Year 11 lesson on employment in the local area, where good presentation, organisation and constant support allowed pupils to complete their task and recall the main points.

Does the school provide effectively for work-related education, including careers education and guidance?

You should evaluate how far pupils have opportunities to learn 'about work', 'through work' and 'for work'. You will have to ensure that the inspection team is deployed in such a way that, as far as possible, work-related aspects of the curriculum are inspected and evidence co-ordinated.

You should evaluate:

- the quality of the curriculum and the extent to which it prepares pupils for the next stage of education;

- the contribution made by school–business partnerships, vocational education, training or employment;

- the contribution made by school subjects and extra-curricular activities;

- how the use of specific resources supports work-related learning;

- the standards of key skills taught (communication, application of number and information technology);

- the quality of teaching and its impact on educational standards achieved.

Does the school have links with the community which contribute to pupils' learning?

Assess the different links the school has established and gauge if the school has done all it can to tap the resources available within its locality and beyond. Access to the Internet and well-developed skills in information and communications technology mean that many pupils now have enriching opportunities to link with others all around the world. Whenever possible evaluate the school's involvement in the wider community, using such things as sporting or cultural events to broaden the experiences offered to pupils. There will be worthwhile visits out of school and interesting visitors, representatives of the community coming in to share their lifestyle and skills with pupils.

Does the school have constructive relationships with partner institutions such as contributory schools?

A special school or PRU with good links will, in line with national policies on inclusion, share expertise and resources and, where relevant to particular pupils, will also:

- draw on and use what the pupils' previous school know about the pupils' attainment;
- familiarise pupils and parents with the expectations and pattern of work in the special schools or PRU before they are admitted;
- collect and use a range of information about pupils' attitudes, values and personal development;
- be clear about pupils' strengths and weaknesses in literacy and numeracy;
- plan return to mainstream schools carefully involving parents and pupils closely;
- inform and prepare mainstream schools and other institutions or placements about transfer through effective liaison;
- provide necessary support and guidance whilst gradually reducing support;
- provide a summary report as pupils transfer back (required for PRUs);

at age 16:

- provide pupils with a survey of their academic and personal achievements as a basis for their future choices;
- provide consistent and impartial advice on what comes next based on a good knowledge of what is available;
- keep track of choices and the progress students make;

at age 18:

- take care to assemble its knowledge of the range and variety of post-18 opportunities, including employment and training;
- provide students with good-quality advice and guidance on future choices, on an individual basis.

☐ How well the school cultivates pupils' personal – including spiritual, moral, social and cultural – development

Your evaluation of the provision for pupils' spiritual, moral, social and cultural development links these four aspects of personal development in which schools have an important part to play. Although each aspect of spiritual, moral, social and cultural development can be viewed separately, the provision is likely to be interconnected and your evaluation should reflect this. Your focus should be on what the school actively does to promote pupils' development in these aspects.

A good deal of your evidence for this section will come from your classroom observations. You need to be alert, therefore, to all situations which contribute to pupils' personal development and make sure you record them on your *Evidence Forms* so that you have a range of examples for possible inclusion in the written report.

Does the school provide pupils with knowledge and insights into values and beliefs, and enables them to reflect on their experiences in a way which develops their spiritual awareness and self-knowledge?

Assess how well the staff provide opportunities that help pupils explore the values of others. Young children will only be able to develop insight into the values and beliefs of others if their own ideas are valued by their parents and teachers. As they get older, this acceptance of their own ideas continues in importance and spreads across all aspects of the curriculum, for example in stories, drama, art, music, history and religious education.

Effective provision for spiritual development depends on a curriculum and teaching methods that embody clear values, and provide opportunities for pupils to gain understanding by developing a sense of curiosity through reflection on their own and other people's lives and beliefs. It relies on teachers receiving and valuing pupils' ideas across the whole curriculum, for example in literature, art, music, history and religious education. Acts of collective worship play a particular part. To the extent that spiritual insights imply an awareness of how pupils relate to others, there is a strong link to both moral and social development. Judge how effectively the school plans for spiritual development as well as how good it is at seizing the moments which arise in everyday life.

Although religious education and spiritual development are not synonymous, religious education can make a significant contribution to spiritual development. Evaluate, for example, whether pupils are encouraged (as far as they can) to:

- consider life's fundamental questions and how religious teaching can relate to them;

- respond to such questions with reference to the teachings and practices of religions as well as from their own experience and viewpoint;

- reflect on their own beliefs or values in the light of what they are studying in religious education.

Collective worship

As far as practicable, special schools should provide a daily act of collective worship, but this does not apply to PRUs. Your evaluation should focus on whether acts of worship are well planned and encourage pupils to explore questions about meaning and purpose, values and beliefs. Compliance with statutory requirements on collective worship should be recorded in *Form S3*.

Taken over a term, the majority of such acts of worship should be wholly or mainly of a broadly Christian character. The school prospectus should make clear the parents' right to withdraw their children from collective worship. In forming a judgement about the character and quality of worship in schools, the following points may be helpful:

- worship is generally understood to imply the recognition of a supreme being. It should be clear that the words used and/or the activities observed in worship recognise the existence of a deity;

- collective worship should not be judged by the presence or absence of a particular ingredient. It might include: sharing values of a Christian nature; opportunities for prayers or meditation; opportunities to reflect upon readings from holy texts or other writings which bring out religious themes; and performance of music, drama and/or dance;

■ each act of worship observed in a school should be considered together before reaching a judgement and then set alongside what is planned over a term. On balance, if it is judged that what the school provides is not in keeping with the spirit of the law, then this should be reported clearly;

■ collective worship may be judged not to fulfil statutory requirements but could still be observed to make a powerful contribution to spiritual, moral, social and cultural development. If this is the case it should be explained in the report.

Does the school promote principles which distinguish right from wrong?

It is a fundamental responsibility of teachers and other adults who work with nursery and primary-age pupils to help them understand the difference between right and wrong. Moral development means that the child's actions are governed by an internalised set of principles and values rather than any fear of sanctions or craving for reward. With support, nursery children are aware of what is acceptable and unacceptable behaviour. Older pupils are able to make moral decisions through the application of reason, even though they may not cope quite so securely with problems in which they are emotionally involved. In other words, their learning about moral issues may be at a different point from their behaviour. Moral and social education are closely related and depend on the school promoting and fostering values such as honesty, fairness and respect for truth and justice.

Evaluate how effectively the school provides a moral code as a basis for behaviour which is promoted throughout the life of the school. Pupils should be given chances to develop and express moral values and extend their personal understanding across a range of issues, including equal opportunities and personal rights and responsibilities. Incidents which arise in school and well-chosen stories may also be useful in teaching morality and behaviour.

Does the school encourage pupils to take responsibility, show initiative and develop an understanding of living in a community?

Schools which are effective in promoting the social development of their pupils provide many opportunities for pupils to take responsibility, show initiative and develop an understanding of living in a community. Whatever the age of the child, social competence hinges on the acceptance of group rules. Learning how to relate to others and to take responsibility for one's own actions is an important part of social education. The quality of the relationships in the school is of crucial importance in forming the pupils' attitudes to good social behaviour and self-discipline.

Adults provide powerful role models for younger children and should, therefore, model the values such as courtesy and respect in all their dealings with other adults and children in the school. Assess how well the adults in the school encourage pupils to work together co-operatively, to compete fairly and to act on their own initiative. Look for the ways in which pupils are helped to take responsibility. For pupils of nursery age it may include taking charge of getting out and putting away resources or caring for living things such as plants or pets. For older pupils, there may be chances to look after younger pupils or run activities such as fundraising. It may also include taking part as a member of a school council, with real opportunities to voice opinions and have them acted on.

You need to consider how the school, through its organisation, curriculum and other activities, contributes to social development through experience and understanding of social relationships and the rights and responsibilities of individuals within the social setting. Evidence may include opportunities for pupils to work co-operatively in lessons, on projects or in games involving competition, discipline and fair play. You should take account of opportunities for pupils to take on responsibility, demonstrate initiative and contribute to the life of the school as a community. Vocational courses at Key Stage 4 and post-16 can play a significant part in this development.

Does the school teach the pupils to appreciate their own cultural traditions as well as the diversity and richness of other cultures?

The school's approach should be active. Look for evidence of how the school promotes the cultural traditions of its own area and the ethnic and cultural diversity of British society. You may see it in something as simple as teaching traditional playground games, or in capitalising on the skills of local artists, workers and residents of the area. Contributions to cultural development can come from all subjects of the curriculum as well as extra-curricular activities. Art, literature and music are often areas where traditions of other cultures can be drawn upon, appreciated and valued. These areas are enriched when the school is able to draw on people from different countries and cultures to share experiences with the pupils.

Example 4.4

Extract from a report (SLD)

Provision for understanding that diversity and richness of other cultures is also good. Multi-cultural awareness is threaded through the curriculum. For example, pupils study the colours and shapes in African art in preparation for creating their own prints, and each music lesson ends by listening to a piece of music, examples of which come from all over the world. Religious education makes a satisfactory contribution to pupils' and students' cultural awareness as they study the customs and beliefs of different people, and look at the origin of their own families. Library books include some featuring lifestyles of other cultures and there are good displays which reflect the traditions and religions of various peoples. The school uses a rich multi-ethnic population of the school as a valuable source of inspiration and information, and this helps pupils and students to appreciate their own cultural traditions.

[Overall: cultural development very good (2)]

5. HOW WELL DOES THE SCHOOL CARE FOR ITS PUPILS OR STUDENTS?

Inspectors must evaluate and report on:

☐ the steps taken to ensure pupils' welfare, health and safety, including the school's arrangements for child protection;

☐ the effectiveness of the school's assessment and monitoring of pupils' academic performance, and monitoring of personal development and attendance;

☐ the effectiveness of the school's educational and personal support and guidance in raising pupils' achievements.

In determining their judgements, inspectors should consider the extent to which the school:

- ensures the health, safety, care and protection of all pupils;

- has effective measures to promote good attendance and behaviour, and to eliminate oppressive behaviour including all forms of harassment and bullying;

- has effective arrangements for assessing pupils' attainments and progress;

- uses its assessment information to guide its planning;

- provides effective support and advice for all its pupils, informed by the monitoring of their academic progress, personal development, behaviour and attendance;

- meets statutory requirements for day and residential provision where relevant or as outlined in a statement of special educational needs;

- has care arrangements for boarding pupils that take account of the Children Act 1989, and as set out in approval regulations and guidance for independent schools.

INSPECTION FOCUS

Focus your inspection on how effectively the school cares for its pupils, whatever their needs or circumstances, not just on the policies and systems. There are three components to the inspection of care and guidance:

■ the welfare and safety and child protection arrangements for pupils;

■ the assessment of pupils' academic and personal development, as well as their attendance;

■ the use of support and guidance to raise pupils' achievement.

Although much of the evidence you gather will be common to all three components, in SHORT INSPECTIONS you are only required to make judgements and report on the first of these, *unless* concerns emerge about the care of pupils. If you are concerned, you will need to explore these further.

In all inspections:

■ give priority to pupils' safety and protection, and in your report summary and commentary state any aspect of care which is a strength or weakness;

■ always report orally any shortcomings in health and safety matters to the governors or the appropriate authority. Do not publish any information that could jeopardise pupils' safety.

If pupils are not well cared for they will not be able to learn effectively. This is particularly true for those pupils who need to board, and depend on the school to provide for their emotional, physical and other personal needs. In PRUs, many pupils may not have attended school regularly and their welfare needs may be high. For pupils with complex and sometimes regressive conditions, the quality of care provided is fundamental to their health, safety, welfare and to their dignity.

From your pre-inspection analysis and initial visit, you already know some of the challenges and issues the school faces. These will give a specific focus to your inspection. In the case of schools with boarding provision, you will need to obtain, prior to the inspection, a copy of the report by the local social services' registration and inspection unit on the school's boarding provision.

MAKING JUDGEMENTS

In SHORT INSPECTIONS, you should take account of all the relevant criteria to come to your judgement about whether pupils' welfare is safeguarded, even though you are not required to report on them. This ensures that all aspects of welfare are considered.

The following characteristics illustrate where to pitch judgements. When your evidence for how well the school cares for its pupils contains these or similar features you should make judgements along the following lines.

Very good or excellent	Teachers know individual pupils very well, and are fully aware of their physical, emotional and intellectual needs. They respond to them in a positive and developmental way. The day-to-day work of the school, in terms of supervision, awareness of hazards and the promotion of healthy living, creates a strong sense of the importance of health and safety of pupils. The school has effective practices to identify how well pupils are making progress, particularly in the core subjects and personal, social and health education and the achievements of different groups. This identification is followed by good diagnosis of what such groups do well and how they might improve. The school has effective ways of being aware of developing patterns in pupils' behaviour or attendance and relating these to patterns of achievement. The systematic monitoring of pupils leads to, for example, changes or modifications to the curriculum or to individual support for pupils' performance and development.
Satisfactory or better	Teachers know pupils well, recognise their needs and respond well to them. The working environment is safe and pupils are well supervised at work and at play. The school maintains accurate records of pupils' achievements in the core curriculum and personal, social and health education and these are well used in order to monitor progress and guide teaching. The school promotes good behaviour and attendance through agreed, shared and successfully implemented policies. The monitoring the school carries out of pupils' performance and development is used to make changes in approach and emphasis.

The school's care of its pupils **cannot be satisfactory** if:

- it does not take reasonable steps to ensure the care of individual pupils and minimise the possibility of significant harm;

- it does not satisfactorily track the progress of pupils in English and mathematics, in personal, social and health education and through its care arrangements, and take action to raise achievements;

- it does not adequately monitor and deal with problems of behaviour and attendance.

REPORTING REQUIREMENTS

SUMMARY REPORT	On all inspections you must complete the box, HOW WELL DOES THE SCHOOL CARE FOR ITS PUPILS OR STUDENTS?, in the table headed OTHER ASPECTS OF THE SCHOOL with comments on any particular strengths and weaknesses.
	If any of these are a feature of improvement in the school, record this in the section HOW THE SCHOOL HAS IMPROVED SINCE ITS LAST INSPECTION.
	Any aspects that are particularly good or need to improve should be reported under WHAT THE SCHOOL DOES WELL or WHAT COULD BE IMPROVED.
SHORT INSPECTIONS	Expand in the commentary any parts from WHAT THE SCHOOL DOES WELL or WHAT COULD BE IMPROVED.
FULL INSPECTIONS	Report under the heading HOW WELL DOES THE SCHOOL CARE FOR ITS PUPILS OR STUDENTS?

On FULL INSPECTIONS, assessment and monitoring of pupils' academic performance and monitoring of personal development and attendance **must be considered unsatisfactory** if:

- the school is ineffective in assessing the pupils' attainments and does not track their progress in core subjects;

- the school does not effectively monitor pupils' personal development;

- the school does not adequately monitor and promote attendance, and does not take effective steps to reduce unauthorised absence.

On FULL INSPECTIONS, the effectiveness of the school's educational and personal support and guidance **must be considered unsatisfactory** if:

- the support and guidance to pupils fails to give attention to raising pupils' achievements and improving behaviour and attendance.

GUIDANCE ON USING THE CRITERIA

The following guidance provides further details for each of the criteria. Refer to these as appropriate to your inspection in the context of the particular school.

☐ **The steps taken to ensure pupils' welfare, health and safety, including the school's arrangements for child protection**

Does the school ensure the health, safety, care and protection of all pupils?

The quality of care is evident in *all* the relationships in the school, in teachers' knowledge of children and their needs and how the school acts to promote the best interests of all individual pupils. Be aware of the principles which govern the Children Act and check whether they are understood by the school. These are that the school should:

■ work in pupils' best interests to safeguard their welfare and promote their development;

■ intervene to protect pupils from harm when necessary;

■ work in partnership with other responsible agencies to secure pupils' welfare;

■ consider the wishes and feelings of those with parental responsibility;

■ give due consideration to the child's religion, racial origin, cultural and linguistic background.

Pupils' welfare and safety are reflected in the quality of care they receive and the effectiveness of the school's arrangements to:

■ ensure that each child is well known by at least one teacher, who links effectively with staff with key responsibilities in the school;

■ ensure that all children and staff work in a safe environment;

■ ensure child protection arrangements comply with procedures that are agreed locally;

■ promote good attendance;

■ promote good behaviour which is free from harassment and bullying;

■ identify and meet individual needs;

■ promote healthy and safe living.

In all inspections, the data provided by the school will give you a starting point for your further investigations. For example, the data on attendance and exclusions, and information from the headteacher's statement in *Form S4*, will give you important indicators.

When you walk around the school judge the safety of the environment for pupils and staff:

■ ask about the day-to-day working practices to ensure that pupils and staff are protected from harm;

■ check the health and safety policy is regularly monitored;

■ check the quality of supervision of children during playtime, and before and after school.

Good schools will successfully build on their day-to-day arrangements in complying with procedures adopted by the local Area Child Protection Committee (ACPC). You should check whether:

■ staff are aware who is the designated senior member of staff responsible;

■ the school policy is in line with local procedures;

- staff are aware of what to do if they suspect, or have disclosed to them, that an individual child may need protection;

- the designated senior member of staff has detailed knowledge of local procedures;

- staff know who the LEA's responsible officer is;

- staff have knowledge of the possible signs and symptoms of child abuse;

- new staff are informed about what to do as part of their induction;

- all staff receive in-service training to maintain and update their knowledge and understanding of the procedures.

Find out how the school liaises with other agencies in monitoring the progress of pupils on the 'at risk' register. For example, find out the arrangements for attending case conferences and for providing reports at the request of the ACPC on how individual children are getting on at school. In addition, you will find evidence in the school's curriculum to judge how the pupils are helped to look after themselves and to develop a responsible attitude as they grow up. If you find a school does not have effective procedures complying with those of the ACPC, explain any mis-match when it occurs. This must be reported to the headteacher and the appropriate authority and included in the inspection report.

You will need to evaluate how successfully the school cares for pupils who are known to need particular attention and for whom the school needs to be especially vigilant. The school has a duty, for example, to ensure that the provision outlined in statements of SEN is implemented. The provision may require liaison with external SEN support staff and other agencies such as health authorities and social services departments. Other pupils with dietary or medical problems, or difficult home circumstances, may require the school to take particular care. Find out how well aware the school is of any pupils 'looked after' by the local authority, and how sensitively staff who need to know the particular circumstances liaise with carers.

In an effective school, staff will know in detail about the different needs of pupils and will provide consistent and convincing responses to your questions about what they do to help pupils, and how pupils are assisted to look after themselves. Look at the impact the personal, social and health education programme has in enabling pupils to be increasingly independent, self-confident and knowledgeable about themselves and healthy and safe living. If the school is part of the government's 'healthy school' initiative you should be able to trace and evaluate the impact of this participation in the day-to-day work of the school. Look, for example, at how the school teaches younger pupils to remember their home address or telephone number in case they are lost, and how, in liaison with the police, they deal with strangers whom they may encounter.

Does the school have effective measures to promote good attendance and behaviour, and to eliminate oppressive behaviour such as all forms of harassment and bullying?

The priority staff give to encouraging good attendance and behaviour is a strong indicator of the steps taken by the school to ensure pupils' welfare and safety. Do teachers encourage individual pupils to attend and be punctual, and is this backed up in assemblies, which are often occasions when the whole school is reminded about attendance? You may have picked up from the parents' questionnaire, or at the meeting before the inspection, how the school encourages parents to ensure their child's attendance. In special schools and PRUs where it is an issue, you should check how incidents of truancy or absconding are handled, particularly noting how the number of incidents is kept to a minimum.

For primary-age pupils much of the responsibility for reminding pupils about how to behave well, and about their attitudes to others, rests with class teachers. Look at the evidence of teaching to determine how successfully teachers minimise disruption and poor behaviour through their skilful handling of pupils in lessons and help pupils know what behaviour is expected of them. You should assess the impact of the school's statutory behaviour policy in promoting respect and tolerance towards others and their beliefs, cultures and ethnic backgrounds.

Check that the policy makes clear the school's intolerance of bullying and racial and sexual harassment. Check there are policies for recording the pattern and frequency of racial incidents and that such incidents and the actions taken are reported annually to the appropriate authority, parents and the LEA. See how consistently staff reward pupils for good work and behaviour in and outside the school, and, when there is poor behaviour, that sanctions are also consistently and appropriately used in proportion to the misdemeanours.

In special schools or PRUs, which serve pupils with emotional or behavioural difficulties, a key feature of the provision is what staff do when pupils' behaviour causes them concern. Check the incident book, which should preferably be bound with numbered pages, is up to date and used to promote better behaviour. Also with regard to sanctions, a punishment book is similarly organised and maintained where this is a mandatory requirement (this includes approved independent schools). You should also check that when restraint is used, it is logged carefully and separately from the punishment and incident books. All staff concerned should have received appropriate guidance and in-service training. Check that their practice conforms to local guidelines and national guidance in Curricular 10/98 (issued under Section 550A of the Education Act 1996) and, where applicable, to the Department of Health and DfEE guidance on permissible forms of restraint.

Your observations around the school in lessons, and discussions with pupils, will help you evaluate how the school eliminates oppressive behaviour, bullying and harassment. Ask for the records of any incidents that have taken place during the previous 12 months. Take particular note of the measures the school takes to prevent bullying, harassment and racial incidents, and whether, in your view, they are working. Check that no groups or individuals are unfairly treated and disadvantaged.

☐ **The effectiveness of the school's assessment and monitoring of pupils' academic performance, and monitoring of personal development and attendance**

Does the school have effective arrangements for assessing pupils' attainments and progress? Does it use its assessment information to guide its planning?

In FULL INSPECTIONS you should evaluate how effective the school is in assessing how well pupils are doing academically and how well they are developing in their personal skills.

In special schools, you should evaluate the effectiveness of the school's arrangements for assessing pupils' attainment through the individual target setting procedures as well as any subject-based assessment. For many pupils, particularly those with severe or profound and multiple learning difficulties, assessment is likely to be primarily an ongoing process, recording the responses and reactions to the work undertaken. Priority should be given to key targets in communication skills, personal, social skills and life-skills including numeracy, and reflect the particular needs of the pupils. Find out how well the school assesses very small gains in attainment and how well the recording systems are organised to enable staff to note efficiently and consistently what pupils know, understand and can do.

Where National Curriculum tests and teacher assessments are used judge how effective the internal moderation procedures are in ensuring that there is consistent practice and that they conform to criteria required by the Qualifications and Curriculum Authority (QCA).

Example 5.1

> **Extract from an inspector's Notebook (2–19 SLD school)**
>
> *IEPs in early years classes are precise and state performance to be attained by end of term – e.g., (from CR's IEP – receptive language) – 'will identify and give item which is blue, red, green or yellow from mixed collection' (S). [EFs 4, 9,10]*
>
> *These EY IEPs inform lesson planning – example above is reflected in English planner for this week – LSA to work with CR on colours (S). [EFs 3, 4, 7, 21]*
>
> *IEPs for post-16 largely cross-refer to selected Youth Award Scheme targets; these are objective and reviewed systematically as part of the scheme (S). [EFs 18,19]*
>
> *IEPs in KS1–4:*
>
> - *are too vague in terms of outcome and timescale, e.g., KS1 'work towards clearer speech in social situations'; KS3 'develop letter formation'. These defeat attempts at review and evaluation at the end of the term (W). [EFs 8,16,18]*
>
> - *or fail to refer to pupils' performance, e.g. KS2 'join percussion group Wednesday pms' (W). [Efs 11, 17, 27]*
>
> - *are not reviewed effectively and tend to be repeated term after term – e.g., JW in Class 6 'work on number patterns' repeated for four terms [EF 14].*
>
> *Practice in EY and post-16 needs to be disseminated through school.*
>
> *Discussed with ARR co-ordinator [EF 30] – aware of differences but unsure how to raise KS1–4 quality. Headteacher aware of contrasts but accepts the situation – 'teacher's personal styles of planning'.*
>
> *[Contributes to judgement that IEPs are poor (6)]*

You should note that PRUs are not obliged to undertake National Curriculum assessment. Your judgement on the effectiveness of assessment in PRUs should take account of:

- effective use of IEPs, where these are produced for pupils in line with the SEN Code of Practice;

- the requirement on PRUs to report on pupils when they are transferred back to mainstream or special schools or for pupils over 16 years when they leave school;

- the requirement to keep parents well informed of pupils' progress.

The progress of pupils attending the PRU should be included in an annual report to the LEA. Some units may use Records of Achievement as a way of gathering information, when pupils move on to their next stage. Your judgements should take account of the paramount need for teachers to keep well informed about pupils' progress because of the short-term nature of the provision.

Judge how well teachers assess pupils in all aspects of their work, behaviour and personal development so that they have a full picture of their pupils' strengths and weaknesses. This should include qualities such as persistence, application, co-operation with others, ability to concentrate, and self-confidence. See if the teacher assesses how well individual pupils behave in different contexts, for example in lessons where pupils are encouraged to investigate individually or in groups, or in physical education and sports. Check how well co-ordinators and assessment co-ordinators work together with teachers so that consistent records are produced and used throughout the school to guide planning and improve achievement.

Judge how well the school monitors the results of its assessments so as to identify the achievements of different ethnic groups by ability or by gender. Check how well this information is recorded and analysed (particularly in providing support for EAL) to help the school take action to improve achievement. If there is no evidence of monitoring the achievement of different groups of pupils, it raises questions about how effective the school is in meeting the needs of all the pupils.

Look at how the school monitors its attendance and analyses the attendance data. Do teachers understand what constitutes authorised absence? How consistent are they in recording unauthorised absence? Check how patterns of truancy or absconding are noted and acted upon.

Judge how well the behaviour policy is reviewed if exclusions take place, and if the appropriate authority was properly involved, and what action the school takes to review its practice, if necessary. Parents should be kept informed about the behaviour policy at least annually.

Example 5.2

Extract from a PRU report

The procedures for monitoring pupils' progress and personal development while they are in the unit are very good. Staff know the pupils very well. They offer them good support in lessons and in the playground, ensuring that they are settled and make progress. Targets set for pupils in their individual education plans and in lessons are clear and realistic and ensure that pupils can achieve progress and see the result of this for themselves. Teachers use formal testing and assessment methods to monitor pupils' progress during the time that they are in the unit but they also use more informal daily assessment, through the good use of questioning and marking of pupils' work, to assess pupils' progress and set daily targets for them to achieve. The home–school diaries are used very well by all staff to record a pupil's achievement, attitudes to learning, behaviour and the quality of work they have achieved during the day, and enable staff to see how a pupil's progress and personal development has improved over time. Pupils' personal development is also very effectively promoted through the use of task and self-assessment sheets where they can assess what they have done well and how they can improve. The individual education plans are of good quality and set clear, attainable targets to ensure that pupils make progress. The reporting of this progress to parents in diaries and in termly reports is detailed and involves them very well in the promotion of positive attitudes to learning.

☐ **The effectiveness of a school's educational and personal support and guidance in raising pupils' achievements**

Does the school provide effective support and advice for all its pupils, informed by the monitoring of their academic progress, personal development, behaviour and attendance?

In FULL INSPECTIONS, your judgement on how effectively the school supports pupils to raise their achievements relies on what you have already found out about assessment practice and the use made of assessment. What does the school do to acknowledge pupils' achievements, particularly when great strides in progress have taken place? Evaluate the effect this has on encouraging all pupils to achieve more.

Find out and assess how well the school identifies what action it can take to help individuals or groups of pupils, for example through changes to the day-to-day organisation and through the provision of extra help. See how well the school discusses what it knows about pupils' strengths and weaknesses with pupils themselves, and with parents and other agencies. Much emphasis will be placed on how well pupils achieve in communication skills. Assess how carefully the school deals with pupils who need to improve their skills in communication and how, in liaison with parents, they are encouraged, yet challenged, to improve. Check that the targets are clear and can be monitored for success. Assess if the school strikes the right balance between doing the best it can, within its resources, before asking for outside help. Make sure the school discriminates between those occasions where outside agencies must be asked for help (for example, child protection) and where it is reasonable for the school to provide support internally.

In PRUs, because of the short-term nature of the provision, educational support and personal guidance should be an intrinsic part of individual plans to deal with immediate needs and to prepare for future provision elsewhere. This should be underpinned by the individual records of academic attainment, particularly in the core subjects, but also in personal and social development, behaviour and attendance. The staff are likely to have responsibility for a small number of pupils and have time to work with them on an individual basis. Pupils themselves should be well briefed about their performance and about their future plans. In some PRUs, the work staff do in helping pupils to improve their behaviour and attendance will be a critical feature of this provision. Check how well staff make use of information about attendance and set realistic targets for improvement. Similarly for behaviour, evaluate how effectively staff help pupils to consider their behaviour in their previous schools, and face the challenge of moving on elsewhere or back to their school or college, rather than allowing pupils to become used to the very different circumstances found in a PRU.

Does the school meet the statutory requirements for day and residential provision as outlined in statements of special educational needs?

Your pre-inspection work on the characteristics of the school should alert you to the particular needs of the pupils. Evidence from the section on HOW GOOD ARE THE CURRICULAR AND OTHER OPPORTUNITIES OFFERED TO PUPILS? should help you in making this judgement. You must make sure that you scrutinise and evaluate a sample of pupils' statements representative of pupils' age and disability. You should check that the statements or reviews are up to date so that you know that the provision outlined in the statement is implemented by the school and any other agency involved, such as speech therapists or LEA support staff. Any evident shortfall in the provision should be further checked to find out why this is so. Ensure that specific disability-related aids for hearing, seeing, writing, to facilitate mobility or for specific arrangements in respect of personal hygiene are available. Check that there is additional staffing, if indicated in the statement, and that it is used effectively. Make sure that specific curricular arrangements are met, such as work in developing communication skills, and that, overall, pupils have their entitlement to a broad and balanced curriculum. Check that arrangements specified in the statement for ensuring that pupils have full access to the whole of the school's curriculum are effective. Where residential provision is specified, check that the arrangements provided by the school match the statement, particularly in respect of the number of nights boarding, regularity of contact with pupils' parents or carers, and specified programmes, for example to boost independence or self-care skills. You need to be sure that there are suitable arrangements to enable all key members of staff who need to know the provision are aware of the contents of the statement and care plan and are able subsequently to contribute to any review that takes place. Attend, if possible, an annual or transition review to ensure that the provision is re-examined in the light of any progress made and that key people attend.

In PRUs, the curriculum provided for pupils who have statements of special educational needs and where the provision relates to other schools should reflect the requirements of those statements as far as it is practicable to do so. As with all pupils, a placement should not be planned other than for the short term. You should consider whether a suitable education is provided by taking account of the special educational needs outlined in the statement and that there are plans for reviewing the provision.

Do the care arrangements for boarding pupils take account of the Children Act 1989 and as set out in approval regulations and guidance for independent schools?

You must evaluate how effectively:

- the school safeguards pupils' welfare and protects them from harm in the residential setting;

- the school supports childcare staff to meet the needs of individual pupils by preparing and implementing care plans;

- the school helps individual pupils to develop emotionally, socially and physically so they can benefit educationally;

- the school provides healthy and nutritious food and looks after pupils' medical needs;

- the school protects pupils by the vetting and supervision of staff, and the provision of well-understood and effective arrangements for pupils to complain, and to have direct and unfettered access to outside help if required;

- pupils have sufficient privacy, appropriate to age and needs, in well-maintained and suitable accommodation;

- pupils have regular opportunities to make personal choices, for example in their clothing and leisure activities.

You should check that the ethos of the boarding provision is such that pupils feel secure, valued and respected as individuals and are able to thrive. Relationships between pupils, and between staff and pupils should reflect this ethos. Opportunities should be available for pupils to gain in self-esteem by the provision of planned activities and opportunities to gain independence. They should be helped to show concern for others and to accept responsibility as they grow older, in preparation for adult life. You should check that the use of sanctions and rewards is appropriate to the pupils and is consistent and fair in its implementation, and especially that schools do not use measures such as withdrawal of food or dressing children differently as forms of punishment, which are expressly forbidden in the Children Act. You should check that staffing levels are sufficient to provide the necessary supervision and support, according to needs. Where appropriate, provision should be available for drugs and sex education, and in dealing with the consequences of sexual and other physical or emotional abuse. Staffing should be sufficient to promote links with families and other important people in pupils' lives, particularly when they live some distance from the school or stay at school for most of the year.

You should evaluate the impact of the care policy in providing effective and consistent practice, for example that:

- each child is known well by one childcare member of staff (for example, through a named person);

- care plans are clear, regularly reviewed (at least every six months if social services departments are involved or annually otherwise), and directly involve the child and family;

- childcare staff have good relations with pupils, appropriate to age and in different contexts (e.g., one-to-one leisure time and when pupils get up or go to bed);

■ childcare staff liaise well with teaching staff, through planned handover procedures and written communication in care plans and other records co-ordinating care and educational planning;

■ the school provides night-waking staff where applicable or nursing staff where children have very specific medical needs;

■ childcare staff contribute appropriately to each child's six-monthly or annual review.

6. HOW WELL DOES THE SCHOOL WORK IN PARTNERSHIP WITH PARENTS?

Inspectors must evaluate and report on:

☐ parents' views of the school;

☐ the effectiveness of the school's links with parents;

☐ the impact of the parents' involvement with the work of the school.

In determining their judgements, inspectors should consider the extent to which:

- parents are satisfied with what the school provides and achieves;

- parents are provided with good quality information about the school, and particularly about pupils' progress;

- links with parents, including the use of home–school agreements, contribute to pupils' learning at school and at home.

INSPECTION FOCUS

Parents depend on the school to provide well for their children. You need to find out whether they feel the school lives up to their expectations and responds to any concerns.

Where a school uses the OFSTED parents' questionnaire you will be able to evaluate how parents feel about the main aspects of the school. You need to use your professional judgement as to the number of responses to a question that signify an important strength or weakness as perceived by parents. The responses to the questionnaire will indicate where you may need more information and issues you may want to follow up at the parents' meeting.

The best opportunity for parents to share their views with you comes at the meeting for parents who have children at the school. Use this meeting:

- to explore the views of parents on those aspects of the school specified in the inspection schedule;

- to follow up issues from the parents' responses to the questionnaire;

- to allow parents to tell you what they think about the school;

- to judge whether there are groups of parents who have not been heard and provide an opportunity for their views to be heard.

There are many other opportunities for you to find out what parents think of the school. For instance:

- parents may request to see you or speak to you on the telephone during an inspection;

- talking with parents who work and help in the school;

- talking with parents at the beginning and the end of the school when they bring and collect their children;

- by visiting events held for parents during the period of the inspection;

- parents of pupils who board should be encouraged to write or speak on the telephone.

On SHORT INSPECTIONS, you are only required to follow up the areas relating to issues raised by parents' views that seem from the parent meeting and questionnaire to be important.

On FULL INSPECTIONS, evaluate also how well the school involves parents as partners in their children's learning; and the quality and effectiveness of the information it provides for parents, and particularly the effect these have on improving pupils' achievements, including their personal development.

Evaluate how well the school consults parents about its curriculum provision and about major spending decisions. This will tell you about the application of the principle of consultation within the best value framework.

MAKING JUDGEMENTS

To make your judgements, use all the evidence you have about the parents' level of satisfaction with the school, the effectiveness of the school's partnership with them and the contribution that this partnership makes to pupils' learning.

Consider this evidence alongside the evidence and judgements that you have made in HOW WELL DOES THE SCHOOL CARE FOR ITS PUPILS? In particular, examine those judgements you have made on the effectiveness of support and advice provided by the school for its pupils and how well parents are able to use this information to help their children learn.

The following characteristics illustrate where to pitch judgements about how well the school works in partnership with parents and carers.

Very good or excellent	The school has a good range of productive and consistent links with parents which help pupils learn. The mechanisms for exchanging information between school and home are effective and include opportunities for parents to give information to the school about their child. Individual target setting is well understood by parents because the school involves them as much as possible. Information to parents through written reports and annual reviews are of good quality, making clear what pupils need to do to improve and how parents can help. There is strong parental satisfaction within the school, based on secure understanding and regular involvement in its work. There is evidence of improvement in children's learning, behaviour and personal development resulting from good liaison with parents.
Satisfactory or better	The school has effective links with parents to consolidate and extend pupils' learning. Parents are, in the main, satisfied with the standards achieved and what the school provides, with no major concerns. Reports to parents and annual reviews are clear and useful, and the exchange of information is sound.

However, the partnership with parents **cannot be satisfactory** if:

- there is a significant degree of dissatisfaction among parents about the school's work, which is supported by inspection findings;

- information to parents does not give a clear view of children's progress, particularly in English and mathematics, and personal social and health education;

- parents are kept at arm's length and the school makes little effort to communicate with them and involve them in the life of the school.

REPORTING REQUIREMENTS

SUMMARY REPORT

All inspectors must complete the table headed PARENTS' VIEWS OF THE SCHOOL, and state the extent to which the inspection team agrees with parents' views. If the school's work with parents is a feature of improvement in the school, record this in the section HOW THE SCHOOL HAS IMPROVED SINCE ITS LAST INSPECTION.

Any aspect that is particularly good or needs to improve should be reported under WHAT THE SCHOOL DOES WELL and WHAT COULD BE IMPROVED.

SHORT INSPECTIONS

Only parents' views of the school are reported. Expand any points made in the commentary under WHAT THE SCHOOL DOES WELL and WHAT COULD BE IMPROVED.

FULL INSPECTIONS

Report under the schedule heading HOW WELL DOES THE SCHOOL WORK IN PARTNERSHIP WITH PARENTS?

GUIDANCE ON USING THE CRITERIA

☐ **Parents' views of the school**

Are parents satisfied with what the school provides and achieves?

You are seeking to establish how far parents are satisfied with the quality and effectiveness of what the school provides and achieves. Decide whether the inspection evidence supports or refutes the views of parents and why. These judgements must then be reported in the summary and, as appropriate, in Part B of the report.

On SHORT INSPECTIONS, you are unlikely to have much time for more detailed work on the quality of the partnership between parents and the school, although where you do find evidence, for instance when examining information provided by the school for parents, you may want to take it into account. On SHORT INSPECTIONS, you should only follow up those areas of the school's relationship with parents that seem from the meeting and questionnaire to be burning issues or that shed important light on what the school does well or not so well.

☐ **The effectiveness of the school's links with parents**

☐ **The impact of parents' involvement with the work of the school**

Are parents provided with good-quality information about the school, and particularly about pupils' progress?

On a FULL INSPECTION, you must evaluate the effectiveness and impact of the school's partnership with parents. The good school sees parents as a rich resource with an important contribution to make and helps parents to support their children's learning. The way in which the school does this, and the extent to which the school and parents work together will have an effect on how well pupils make progress in school.

You must evaluate the extent to which the school actively draws in all parents including those from minority ethnic backgrounds, especially those who do not speak English as a first language, and encourages them to support their children's learning. Your starting point and the source of issues you wish to pursue will be the parents' responses to the questionnaire and their contributions to the parents' meeting. Further evidence will emerge from:

■ talking with parents before and after school;

■ meeting with parents who work and help in the school and on school visits and finding out how the school 'trains' and prepares parents who are involved;

■ talking with parent governors and any representatives from parents' associations and clubs;

■ how far information provided for parents can be understood and used;

■ how well the school keeps in touch with parents who have little English.

Example 6.1

> ### Extract from report on links with parents (SLD school)
>
> *Pupils' and students' annual academic reports are of indifferent quality. Some fail to inform parents adequately of what their children know, understand and can do. However, the reports that accompany each young person's annual review of their statement of special educational needs, and their individual education plan, more than compensate, and provide parents with a comprehensive and accessible picture of their children's progress. These are significant improvements since the previous inspection and are appreciated by parents.*
>
> *Parents' consultation meetings twice a year, parental participation in their child's annual review, and the school's open-door policy ensure a good level of parental involvement in their children's education. Home–school diaries are generally well used, although parents report that this varies according to different teachers, and the school nurse and social worker are in regular contact with families. Parents are consulted on appropriate matters, such as the forthcoming consultation on the draft homework policy, and feel that the school is very responsive to their suggestions and complaints. Specialists in English as a second language assist some parents in understanding the school's written communications. Some parents feel that they would like more immediate information, for example on what items were bought or cooked in food technology, or if a member of staff is ill. On balance, communication with parents is good.*
>
> [Communications with parents good (3) and a good example of best value]

Do links with parents, including the use of home–school agreements, contribute to pupils' learning at school and at home?

An effective partnership includes the sharing of information about children, their learning and how they feel about school. If any visits are made to children and parents before children enter school, evaluate the impact of these on both the parents and children. Find out whether induction programmes are flexible enough to suit the needs of all children. Evaluate the extent to which parents with toddlers and babies are encouraged to come into school, and how easy it is for parents to borrow books and other resources for children. Examine the effectiveness of arrangements for contacts with pupils' homes, to identify and help children who are unhappy, and for involving parents who rarely come near the school.

Assessing the quality of information provided for parents is one part of this evaluation. Areas for enquiry include, for example:

- any policies on home–school contracts and the extent to which they work;

- what account the school takes of what parents know about their own child's learning;

- how far parents and teachers can talk informally together about children, and the arrangements that are made for parents whose first language is not English;

- whether parents are regularly contacted and consulted about their child's individual targets;

- whether reports to parents about pupils' progress tell them clearly what their children are doing, how well they are doing it, whether it is good enough and what they need to do to improve;

- to what extent written reports are followed up and discussed with parents;

- the extent to which pupils' reports and records incorporate the views of parents and show the action agreed to help pupils learn;

- how well the school helps parents to understand what is taught;

- the extent to which any home–school agreements contribute to pupils' learning;

- the extent to which parents know about and use lending libraries for toys and books;

- how well the school communicates with parents who have disabilities, learning difficulties or who live a long way from the school without easy transport;

- how well the school consults parents about its curriculum and about major spending decisions within its application of the consultation principle in the best value framework.

7. HOW WELL IS THE SCHOOL LED AND MANAGED?

Inspectors must evaluate and report on:

- [ ] how efficiently and effectively the headteacher and key staff lead and manage the school, promoting high standards and effective teaching and learning;

- [ ] how well the governing body (or appropriate authority) fulfils its statutory responsibilities and accounts for the performance and improvement of the school;

- [ ] how effectively the school monitors and evaluates its performance, diagnoses its strengths and weaknesses and takes effective action to secure improvements;

- [ ] the extent to which the school makes the best strategic use of its resources, including specific grants and additional funding, linking decisions on spending to educational priorities;

- [ ] the extent to which the principles of best value are applied in the school's use of resources and services;

- [ ] the adequacy of staffing, accommodation and learning resources, highlighting strengths and weaknesses in different subjects and areas of the curriculum where they affect the quality of education provided and standards achieved.

In determining their judgements, inspectors should consider the extent to which:

- leadership ensures clear direction for the work and development of the school, and promotes high standards;

- the school has explicit aims and values, including a commitment to good relationships and equality of opportunity for all, which are reflected in all its work;

- there is rigorous monitoring, evaluation and development of teaching;

- there is effective appraisal and performance management;

- the school identifies appropriate priorities and targets, takes the necessary action, and reviews progress towards them;

- there is a shared commitment to improvement and the capacity to succeed;

- governors fulfil their statutory duties in helping to shape the direction of the school and have a good understanding of its strengths and weaknesses;

- educational priorities are supported through careful financial management;

- good delegation ensures the effective contribution of staff with management responsibilities;

- effective use is made of new technology, including ICT;

- specific grant is used effectively for its designated purpose(s);

- the number, qualifications and experience of teachers and support staff match the demands of the curriculum;

- the accommodation allows the curriculum to be taught effectively;

- learning resources are adequate for school's curriculum and range of pupils;

- there is effective induction of staff new to the school and the school is, or has the potential to be, an effective provider of initial teacher training;

- the best value principles of comparison, challenge, consultation and competition are applied in the school's management and use of services and resources.

INSPECTION FOCUS

Good schools are led and managed for the benefit of all their pupils. Your inspection must focus on the extent to which leadership and management create an effective and improving school where pupils are keen and able to learn. You must evaluate impact rather than intention. You must also ensure that your judgements on the effectiveness of leadership and the efficiency of management make sense when set against your judgements about standards, teaching and learning, and other aspects of the school covered in the *Evaluation Schedule*.

In all inspections focus on:

■ the effectiveness of leadership and the efficiency of management as distinctive elements, provided by the headteacher or teacher in charge, staff with management responsibilities, and governors or the proprietor or members of the management group;

■ the effect of leadership and management on the quality and standards of education;

■ how well the school understands its strengths and weaknesses through its own monitoring and evaluation;

■ the school's commitment to improvement;

■ the appraisal and performance management of the headteacher and other staff.

In SHORT INSPECTIONS, where the school is usually very effective, evaluate why it is and find out what the leaders and managers do that works.

Note: The guidance on the aspects of management, particularly performance management, will be amended as further details become available about the implementation of the 1998 Green Paper.

MAKING JUDGEMENTS

Your overall judgements about how well the school is led and managed should take account of *Form S4* and must tie in with what else you have found out about the school. There is usually, but not always, a clear relationship between the standards achieved and the effectiveness of those who lead and manage. Evaluate the extent to which this causality applies.

The following characteristics illustrate where to pitch judgements about how well the school is led and managed.

Very good or excellent	The leader(s) of the school or PRU share a common purpose and put pupils and their achievements first. They build co-operative and co-ordinated teams and use assessment evidence well to set high goals for pupils and challenging targets for the school and for individual staff. Staff are keen to reflect critically on what they can do to improve learning and develop more effective ways of working. The work of the school is fully and thoroughly monitored, particularly the quality of teaching and its impact, and the behaviour of pupils. There is good delegation to staff with management responsibilities and effective follow-up to ensure tasks are completed well. The appropriate authority monitors performance and has a good understanding of the strengths and weaknesses of the school and the challenges it faces, and sets the right priorities for development and improvement. It fulfils statutory duties well in providing a sense of direction for the school, and understands and applies best value principles.
Satisfactory or better	The leadership and management of the school or PRU are clear about its strengths and weaknesses and have established some ways of securing improvements to standards achieved. Teamwork is well established in the main and the school has identified the right tasks for the future. Most staff share a common purpose and have taken steps to make their work more effective. Staff with particular responsibilities are clear about what they are and how they will measure their success. The appropriate authority has a sound sense of the strengths and weaknesses of the school and is working with staff in their efforts to improve. It meets statutory responsibilities.

However, the leadership and management **cannot be satisfactory** if any of these are present:

- there is a significant amount of unsatisfactory teaching;

- there is significant complacency among staff;

- standards in the school are significantly lower than they should be;

- headteacher, or teacher in charge, senior managers and the appropriate authority are largely ineffective and do not know the strengths and weaknesses of the school.

REPORTING REQUIREMENTS

SUMMARY REPORT

In both FULL and SHORT INSPECTIONS complete the table HOW WELL IS THE SCHOOL LED AND MANAGED?

Comment on the strengths and weaknesses in leadership and management and evaluate briefly the extent the school applies the principles of best value.

If any of these are features of improvement in the school report this in the section HOW THE SCHOOL HAS IMPROVED SINCE ITS LAST INSPECTION.

If any aspects of leadership or management are particularly good or need to improve you must report these under WHAT THE SCHOOL DOES WELL or WHAT COULD BE IMPROVED.

In FULL INSPECTIONS you must include a summary judgement about the adequacy of staffing, accommodation and learning resources.

SHORT INSPECTIONS

In the commentary expand your judgements on leadership and management as reported in either WHAT THE SCHOOL DOES WELL or WHAT COULD BE IMPROVED.

FULL INSPECTIONS

Report comprehensively under the heading HOW WELL IS THE SCHOOL LED AND MANAGED?

When reporting on leadership and management in a FULL INSPECTION, your evaluation must reflect all the criteria. The challenge for inspectors is to give a cohesive account rather than rehearsing findings in terms of each criterion, item by item.

GUIDANCE ON USING THE CRITERIA

In all inspections the first evidence for your evaluation comes from your earliest contacts with the school. Use the school's documentation, *Forms S3* and *S4*, the previous inspection report to formulate some of the initial questions and hypotheses about the work and development of the school and the extent to which it promotes high standards and effective teaching and learning.

When using the criteria to make your judgements, you will need to be aware of what is statutorily required in maintained and non-maintained special schools, independent schools which are approved for admitting pupils with statements, and PRUs.

In all types of special schools, including independent schools, the approved arrangements set by the DfEE (*see Form S1*) should be the starting point for your investigations. In the case of maintained special schools, governors share responsibility with the LEA in some matters, for example in agreeing the particular role of the school, when a change in range of needs served is contemplated, or is taking place over time, in accordance with the LEA's SEN policy and in liaison with the DfEE.

Your judgements should, however, focus on what governors or the appropriate authority do, only indicating the LEA's role if there is a particular impact on how the governing body functions.

In PRUs, you should note that the LEA is the appropriate authority, but that a management committee must be set up. This should include local headteachers and an officer with knowledge or experience of working with the young pupils with behavioural difficulties, in addition to other members reflecting the particular type of PRU. For example, a young mother's unit may have a representative from the health authority – such as a health visitor. You should be aware of the committee's responsibilities in implementing the policy of PRU and evaluating the success of the provision in respect of its:

■ admissions and reintegration;

■ discipline;

■ attendance;

■ curriculum;

■ provision for pupils with SEN;

■ action following an inspection.

Check that the teacher in charge of the PRU produces a report at least annually to the management committee.

☐ **How efficiently and effectively the headteacher and key staff lead and manage the school, promoting high standards and effective teaching and learning**

Leadership is concerned with:

■ creating and securing commitment to a clear vision;

■ managing change so as to improve the school;

■ building a high-performing team;

■ inspiring, motivating and influencing staff;

■ leading by example and taking responsibility.

Management is concerned with:

■ strategic thinking and planning;

■ people, including performance management; making best use of the skills of staff; delegation, appraisal and development;

■ financial and other resources;

■ communication;

■ monitoring and evaluating performance and delivering results.

You need to distinguish between leadership and management when considering the operation of the school, although the two overlap.

Do leadership and management ensure a clear direction for the work and development of the school and promote high standards?

Your judgements here must take account of any constraints or opportunities the headteacher or teacher in charge has due to changes in character, re-organisation or, in the case of independent schools, particular conditions with which the head is expected to comply. You should bear in mind that in the case of PRUs the LEA sets the context for the PRU to operate within its policy for 'education otherwise' and that sometimes the professional head of the PRU (or designated headteacher/or teacher in charge) may not be the day-to-day teacher in charge.

You need to establish what the headteacher's or teacher in charge's vision for the school is and how far, together with senior staff, they give a firm steer to the school's work. For example, is the school striving to work with other schools, particularly mainstream, in line with national policies on inclusion? Apply the same perspective to the work of other co-ordinators and evaluate the extent to which the headteacher's or teacher in charge's leadership helps them to do a good job. Development and improvement planning should reflect the school's stated aims and objectives and promote high standards.

The evaluations that you have undertaken so far will enable you to begin to judge what aspects of standards and the success of pupils can be traced back to the impact of the school's leaders and managers. Where there are weaknesses in the work of the school and particularly in what you see in classes, you should track these issues back to see how well the weaknesses are understood by senior staff and what they have done about them.

Does the school have explicit aims and values, including a commitment to good relationships and equality of opportunity for all, which are reflected in all its work?

You will see a great deal in your first contact with the school which brings to life its stated aims and values. Evidence will come from: how the headteacher/teacher in charge, teaching staff and pupils interact with each other; signs of staff and pupils being valued and the school's commitment to inclusive policies; the welcome given to visitors; the quality and care of the school environment; and pride shown in the school by staff and pupils.

In lessons, look for a sense of purpose and signs that what the school and its management stand for are reflected in teaching, for example in the approaches taken to meet the needs of different individual pupils and groups.

Talk to staff and pupils about their views of the school and what it stands for, equal opportunities, and the extent to which senior staff are interested in their work.

Use your evidence from teaching and learning to evaluate how well the school meets the needs of particular groups of pupils. For instance, judge how far the SEN Code of Practice, in schools other than independent schools, is properly implemented and resourced, or how the needs of Traveller children are met.

Is there a shared commitment to improvement and capacity to succeed?

In order to establish the school's commitment to improvements and its capacity to succeed, assess:

- whether or not standards and the expectations of teachers are high enough;

- the headteacher's/teacher in charge's skills of leadership, decision-making and communication;

- how far the headteacher/teacher in charge and senior staff in the school know what needs to be done to improve and how to do it;

- how aware the staff are of what needs to be done, and ways in which they can improve.

Does good delegation ensure the effective contribution of staff with management responsibilities?

If there are strengths or weaknesses in the work of staff with responsibility for co-ordination and development, explain what these are. In smaller schools and particularly in PRUs these responsibilities are sometimes carried informally and staff often hold more than one. Consider the extent to which good delegation ensures the effective contribution of staff with management responsibilities. A good leader ensures that these responsibilities are clearly stated, often in job descriptions, and are effectively carried out. Look for evidence that delegation of work carries specific responsibilities and defined outcomes suited to the needs of the school, and is properly resourced.

In a very effective school, staff, including support staff, know their role in its day-to-day work and longer-term improvement.

Example 7.1

Extract from a report on leadership and management

The headteacher provides very strong leadership and maintains a clear oversight of the work of the school. The deputy headteacher gives able and committed support, and takes responsibility for a number of important aspects, such as the overall management of the curriculum. A significant factor in the success of the school is the way in which responsibilities are delegated. The senior management team and the Key Stage co-ordinators have clear roles, which they understand and fulfil with increasing confidence. Paramount is responsibility for raising standards, for monitoring the achievement of pupils' targets and the evaluation of teaching in the Key Stage. This involves checks on pupils' work and teachers' planning, and visits to classrooms to observe practice. Staff are provided with any necessary training, expectations are clearly defined, and they are then given scope to develop their particular areas. Staff feel involved in the management of the school, and morale is high.

[Contributes to a judgement of very effective leadership and management (1)]

One indication of the headteacher's or teacher in charge's competence and confidence is the way the run up to the inspection has been managed. Has the headteacher or teacher in charge taken it in his or her stride, not allowing it to be too much of a distraction to staff and to the school's work and purpose, or has the inspection prompted unnecessary work and been allowed to induce unnecessary stress? Is the on-site inspection managed well by the school?

☐ **How well the governing body (or appropriate authority) fulfils its statutory responsibilities and is able to account for the performance of the school**

How well do the governors fulfil their statutory duties in helping to shape the direction of the school and do they have a good understanding of its strengths and weaknesses?

The appropriate authority has specific statutory responsibilities and its main tasks are: to provide a sense of direction for the work of the school; to support the work of the school as a critical friend; to hold the school to account for the standards and quality of education it achieves.

The way in which the role of the governing body or other appropriate authority is interpreted may vary significantly in relation to the school size and type, and other factors. Definitions of the role of the governing body (or appropriate authority) are set out in education law; the issue for you is how effectively these roles are interpreted in the context of the particular school. Independent schools do not have a governing body.

In all inspections, your evaluation of the work of the appropriate authority will need to take account of:

- the context of the school and any impact this may have on the balance of skills, competence and commitment found in the work of the appropriate authority;

- the way the appropriate authority ensures that the school meets with statutory requirements;

- the relationship between the work of the headteacher or teacher in charge and senior managers and that of the appropriate authority;

- the extent to which the appropriate authority appraises the work of the headteacher or teacher in charge and sets performance targets for him or her.

Your evidence will come from your discussions with the chair and the members of the governing body or management committee, or the teacher governor representative, the headteacher and staff about:

- the way members exercise their corporate role;

- how well they fulfil their statutory duties;

- how they help to shape the direction of the school;

- their knowledge of the strengths and weaknesses of the school and understanding of the challenges it faces;

- whether appropriate priorities for development and improvement are set;

- how well they have responded to the previous inspection;

- how the appropriate authority find out for themselves how things are going;

- whether or not they take responsibility for good and poor aspects of the school.

Example 7.2

> ### Extract from a report on a pupil referral unit
>
> *The leadership and management of the unit, both by the management group and successive teachers in charge, has been poor. The present teacher in charge has been in post for only a few weeks and has therefore been unable to make significant inroads into some of the problems. Many of the shortcomings flow from the failure of the LEA, as the appropriate authority through its management group, to set and implement action plans to ensure that the purpose of the unit – to re-engage pupils with learning – is met. This key aim is contained in the unit's curriculum statement but is not used sufficiently to influence other plans. It is not clear exactly what part the unit plays in the LEA's provision for Education Otherwise and at school, and therefore what type of pupil should be referred to it. The present criteria for admissions contain some which are clear, such as prolonged or repeated exclusion; some which are not, such as 'Key Stage 4 referral'; and some which are not criteria at all, such as 'looked after children'. The policy is not sufficiently clear to enable those working in the unit to formulate a positive improvement plan. Managers state that the intention is to re-integrate Key Stage 3 pupils into mainstream schools, but not those at Key Stage 4. Although external links, such as with colleges, work-experience providers and the careers service, are good, staff have not thought through their plans for curriculum, assessment or monitoring tracking and aftercare, based on the aim of re-engaging pupils in Key Stage 4 with learning in a college course or in a job with training.*
>
> *The unit admits pupils with a range of problems, including persistent non-attenders; the two are long-term placements, of almost three years' duration; very few pupils re-integrate. Managers believe, and the inspection team agrees, that the unit has on roll a number of pupils who are inappropriately placed.*
>
> *[Contributes to a view that admissions policy is poor (6) and the unit poorly managed (6)]*

☐ **How effectively the school monitors and evaluates its performance, diagnoses its strengths and weaknesses, and takes effective action to secure improvement**

Is there rigorous monitoring, evaluation and development of teaching?

In all inspections you must assess how far and why the school's evaluation of teaching leads to development and improvement. Your starting points will come from *Form S4*, the last report and your judgements of standards and teaching. Look for improvement in teaching in subjects since the last inspection and see if standards are rising. Consider:

- the extent to which teachers are helped to analyse and draw on the approaches which work best with particular pupils;

- how far the school knows and uses the strengths of its best teachers to influence the rest;

- the ways in which the headteacher and other senior staff are involved, and know what is happening, in classrooms;

- whether appraisal of teachers contributes to the monitoring of teaching;

- the extent to which the headteacher's or teacher in charge's view of good and weak teaching is reflected in the work of the school;

- how well the school helps teachers and support staff to work together;

- whether performance targets are set for teachers.

Your evaluation must answer these questions:

- How well does the school monitor and analyse its standards?

- What does it do with the information?

- How well does it evaluate the quality of teaching?

- Does it face up to its weaknesses and take adequate steps to overcome them?

- What impact does all this have?

Is there effective induction of staff new to the school and is the school, or has it the potential to be, an effective provider of initial teacher training?

From September 1999 all newly qualified teachers (NQTs) must have a 90 per cent teaching load, an induction tutor and identified written targets from regular observations. Note that PRUs should not employ teachers in their induction year and regulations prevent the employment of licensed and student teachers at a PRU.

A school could be an effective provider of initial teacher training when:

- it has professional development systems in place that are a good influence on standards of teaching;

- it is judged to be effective overall and to have improved since its previous inspection;

- it has a shared commitment to improvement and the capacity to succeed.

Is there effective appraisal and performance management?

Apart from approved independent schools, the appropriate authority is responsible for ensuring that the headteacher is appraised and targets set, and that the school implements national requirements of the appraisal and pay of teachers. Where you have identified important weaknesses in the performance of teachers these systems are clearly not as effective as they need to be. Evidence of effective systems for managing teachers' performance will be seen when:

- the deployment of resources rewards and motivates good teachers;

- teachers work in harmony towards common goals;

- management problems are tackled squarely;

- capability/competency procedures are used to deal with poor performance;

- there are strategies to reduce staff absence;

- appraisal and regular review assesses performance through classroom observation.

From September 1999 governing bodies have been required to operate an appraisal system for headteachers and to set targets that arise from that appraisal. You will need to evaluate their arrangements for effective appraisal. **Bear in mind any differences in statutory requirements as they apply to non-maintained, independent schools and PRUs.**

Does the school identify appropriate priorities and targets, take the necessary action and review progress towards them?

Effective headteachers identify the right development priorities based on a clear analysis of strengths and weaknesses. In all schools you need to evaluate how far the staff know the right things to do to improve performance and whether or not they do them.

The appropriate authority sets targets for the school, that is establishes specific measurable goals for improved pupil performance. These need to be agreed with the LEA in maintained schools. You must evaluate how well assessment and performance data are used by the school to predict potential, focus effort and support improvement. Schools vary greatly in character and each finds its own particular way to raise achievement. This process is likely to be the most effective if it involves all staff. Where a school knows how good its standards are and how good its teaching is, it is well placed to set targets for itself, take the necessary action and review progress towards them.

Much of your evidence of the effectiveness of target setting will be derived from your evaluation of how well pupils are achieving and making progress. Examine in particular the extent to which:

■ the school makes good use of data on pupils' attainment on entry;

■ information from standardised tests is used effectively;

■ the school questions itself about the performance of different individuals and groups of pupils, and reviews its own current performance against past performance;

■ the school's priorities and targets are appropriate and linked with clear programmes of action;

■ procedures are in place to monitor the outcomes of this work.

☐ **The extent to which the school makes best strategic use of its resources, including specific grants and additional funding, linking decisions on spending to educational priorities**

How well are educational priorities supported through careful financial management?

The funding of special schools will reflect the particular type of school and the range of disabilities it serves. In independent and non-maintained schools, you should check that public funds in the form of individual fees are adequately reflected in the budget allocation which the school has annually. Independent schools have to state their fees in their brochure.

You should find out the cost centre for the PRU and bear in mind the local procedures and pattern of funding when evaluating how well educational priorities are supported by effective financial planning. Similarly you should bear in mind that there might be little data for comparison when evaluating how the PRU conforms to best value principles and there may be little room for manoeuvre in their use of resources.

An efficient school demonstrates that it budgets systematically for all expenditure and is clear about the cost of its development. Your emphasis should not be on the detail of the financial planning, but rather on the extent to which the school's spending decisions relate to priorities for improvement and benefit for pupils. Once priorities have been identified you will need to find out the extent to which the school has applied the best value principles of competition in, for example, obtaining tenders for services or goods *(see Annex 1)*.

Your overriding judgement on the use made by the school of its financial resources and newly developed technologies will be on how far all pupils benefit from wisely targeted spending. Much of the evidence you require for this judgement will be found in lessons.

If you need to investigate further, detailed school information will be found in *Form S2* and must be supplemented by discussion with appropriate staff in the school, particularly the finance officer, where this is not the headteacher. Your evaluation will concentrate on the logic and quality of links between planning and spending.

Another feature of careful financial planning is effective financial control and administration. You are not conducting a detailed financial audit but you must have access to the latest auditors' report. Establish whether:

■ the main recommendations in the report have been acted upon;

■ systems for financial administration are unobtrusive, efficient and responsive to need;

■ financial administration keeps the way clear for teachers to concentrate on their work;

■ adequate information is available to the headteacher and appropriate authority to ensure that finances are kept in good order and costs easily determined.

Example 7.3

The efficiency of the school

Over four years the school has accumulated large budget surpluses. At the beginning of this financial year these surpluses amounted to just over a third of the school's total budget. Part of this sum was a planned reserve to finance capital developments. Nevertheless a substantial amount was an unplanned accumulation of funds arising from unforeseen increases in pupils on roll. The school has taken effective steps to bring the situation under control. The current budget plan provides for a sensible contingency of about 5 per cent. While financial planning is now satisfactory, the many themes for school development are not prioritised. The school has no formal procedures for testing out the cost-effectiveness of the developments it undertakes, which is a weakness.

[Overall: unsatisfactory financial management (5)]

Is effective use made of new technologies, including ICT?

During the inspection ask about the use the school is making of new technologies, including ICT, electronic mail, multimedia compositions, data analysis, CD-ROM, the National Grid for Learning, and Internet applications. Evaluate the role of senior staff in ensuring the effective use of this technology.

Are specific grants used effectively for its designated purpose?

Where a school is in receipt of a specific grant, for instance the Ethnic Minorities Achievement Grant (EMAG), evaluate how well the school is using this money for its designated purpose. Make sure the additional funds are used for their intended purposes by considering:

■ the extent to which the funds are appropriately allocated;

■ how well the school monitors the effectiveness of the spending;

■ whether the outcomes of the expenditure match the objectives;

■ how well the use of additional grants relates to the school's provision, for example for teaching, curriculum and assessment.

☐ **The extent to which the principles of best value are applied in the school's use of services and resources**

To what extent are best value principles of comparison, challenge, consultation and competition applied in the school's management and use of resources?

Detailed guidance on the concepts embodied in best value principles can be found in Annex 1 of this *Handbook*. In all inspections the use the school makes of best value principles must be evaluated.

Schools applying best value principles will recognise the importance of questions such as:

■ How do our standards and costs **compare** with those of other schools?

■ How do we **challenge** ourselves to justify the use of resources to provide educational activities outside the statutory curriculum, for instance parent–school partnerships and vocational courses?

■ How do we satisfy ourselves that **competition** is fair where we buy contracted-out services, for instance school meals?

■ How widely do we **consult**, for example on major spending decisions and changes to the curriculum?

The answers to these questions will tell you how well the school is applying the best value principles.

☐ **The adequacy of staffing, accommodation and learning resources, highlighting strengths and weaknesses in different subjects and areas of the curriculum where they affect the quality of education provided and the educational standards achieved**

Do the number, qualifications and experience of teachers and support staff match the demands of the curriculum?

In FULL INSPECTIONS, only evaluate the extent to which the school is staffed and resourced to teach the curriculum and whether there are any features that contribute to or detract from good quality and high standards. A good school makes the best use of all its available resources to achieve the highest possible standards for all its pupils.

Evaluate how far the staff are qualified to teach the school's curriculum, and are trained or experienced in the appropriate phase, and the extent to which levels of staffing ensure that all pupils are taught effectively. Consider whether there are enough skilled support staff to enable the school to function effectively. Take into account the qualifications and experience of those staff in relation to the needs of the pupils in the school.

When considering the adequacy of the **number, qualifications and experience of teachers and support staff** keep in mind that:

■ staffing in special schools should at least reflect the guidance contained in DES Circular 11/90;

■ in very small special schools and PRUs, particularly those serving a wide age range (say 2–19 years), staffing ratios are likely to be more generous in order to provide the range of activities to meet specific needs, or to provide age-appropriate work;

■ in many schools, nursery assistants and other staff provide complementary support for the work of teachers;

- in an effective team all staff understand their role as well as those of others;

- staff should be trained and experienced to provide the appropriate age-related curriculum;

- every PRU should have a co-ordinator for special educational needs;

In PRUs, there should be at least two members of staff on duty at the PRU base. If they work as part of a wider team, providing support for home tuition or to mainstream schools, they should be adequate in number and employed effectively enough to enable all pupils at the PRU to have access to the broad and balanced curriculum to which they are entitled.

Where the school is affected by staff illness or a pattern of absence comes to your attention, you should evaluate what the school does to support staff and reduce staff absence.

Example 7.4

Extract from a report

The level of effective teaching support provided by trained nursery nurses and special needs assistants is exceptional and makes an enormous contribution to the learning process. Staff have a clear understanding of their own roles and responsibilities which contribute to their highly competent teamwork.

[Overall: excellent teaching support (1)]

Does the accommodation allow the curriculum to be taught effectively? Are learning resources adequate for the school's curriculum and range of pupils?

In inspecting special schools, the adequacy of accommodation may have an important bearing on the range of subjects that can be offered. You should use the guidance in DfEE Building Bulletin 77 and Building Bulletin 84 (mainly about residential accommodation) to make your judgements.

In PRUs you should be aware that there is no requirement for hard play areas and playing fields. PRUs, however, must comply with health, safety and fire regulations and should provide accommodation suitable for its defined purpose, appropriate for providing 'suitable education'. Judgements about accommodation should be made taking into account other opportunities pupils have to learn in other contexts. Pupils should have access to provision for specialist work, including a range of technology, science, and art and crafts. You should judge the adequacy of the PRU accommodation at the base by reference to the maximum number of pupils who are educated there at any one time.

Your evaluation of the adequacy and effectiveness of accommodation and learning resources should be informed by particular strengths and weaknesses identified during the inspection. You should note where provision enhances or detracts from pupils' learning. Evaluate the quality of the accommodation, including outdoor areas, particularly for the younger pupils, and whether they provide a stimulating and well-maintained place for pupils to learn and play. Judge the adequacy and effectiveness of learning resources according to the level of provision, its appropriateness, condition and accessibility. You should judge the effectiveness of the library by the ways in which it promotes higher levels of literacy for all pupils; by the way it is a resource for personal study; by its contribution in encouraging pupils to read widely and confidently; and the extent to which pupils value reading as a source of pleasure and information. Make your judgements and record your **evidence only where provision has a significant impact on standards.**

8. WHAT SHOULD THE SCHOOL DO TO IMPROVE FURTHER?

The report must include:

☐ specific matters – key issues – which the appropriate authority for the school should include in its post-inspection action plan, listed as issues for action in order of their importance in raising standards in the school;

Each issue must be followed by a reference to the main paragraph(s) in the inspection report where the weaknesses are discussed.

These issues should be based on any weaknesses identified in the inspection and include all the matters listed in WHAT COULD BE IMPROVED in relation to **standards** achieved and the **quality of education** provided, with particular emphasis on **teaching**.

Where the inspection highlights issues already identified as priorities in the school's development plan, this section should acknowledge this.

Any non-compliance with statutory requirements where it detracts significantly from the quality and standards of the school, or where it relates to care, health and safety, should be reported here.

☐ a statement indicating paragraphs of the inspection report which refer to other weaknesses, not included in issues for action, but which should be considered by the school.

INSPECTION FOCUS

This section of the report is linked directly to the statements made in the summary under the heading WHAT COULD BE IMPROVED. In that section, you need to summarise the school's main weaknesses, without, at that stage, giving the direction in which the school might move to bring about improvements. The statements included in WHAT SHOULD THE SCHOOL DO TO IMPROVE FURTHER? take that step. They set out what needs to be done to bring about improvement. However, you must not go further than this to indicate how the school could take the required action; that is the proper remit of the appropriate authority and staff. But you must make it absolutely clear what needs to be done, breaking down the statement into several parts if it helps to clarify for the school what it must do.

- ☐ **Specific matters – key issues – which the appropriate authority for the school should include in its post-inspection action plan, listed as issues for action in order of their importance in raising standards in the school**

Each bullet point in the section WHAT COULD BE IMPROVED must, one by one, be covered in this section so that the reader can immediately link each issue for action by the school to an inspection judgement. You must use this section to make it very clear to the school the steps they must take to bring about the improvement that you have identified. This means that you will almost certainly need to use a list format with a number of actions under a heading linked back to the bullet point in WHAT COULD BE IMPROVED.

These key issues should be the big issues for the school, and not matters which are less significant. The detail of this section must naturally lead the school to improvement. A compliance issue should only be included here if it detracts significantly from the quality of the school's provision or the standards that pupils attain. In a SHORT INSPECTION, the level of effectiveness of the school means that it is unlikely that there will be significant compliance issues, but if they do arise they should be indicated here. In a FULL INSPECTION, you should avoid making a long list of compliance issues here unless they are significant.

- ☐ **A statement indicating paragraphs of the report which refer to other weaknesses not included in issues for action, but which should be considered by the school**

In FULL INSPECTIONS only, you should use this statement to bring to the attention of the school those weaknesses which need to be considered by the school but which do not appear as one of the main areas for improvement. You should also use this statement to include compliance issues which, although important, do not significantly detract from the education pupils receive or the standards they achieve.

9. OTHER SPECIFIED FEATURES

Where additional features are specified for inspection, inspectors must evaluate and report on:

☐ the overall effectiveness of each feature.

In determining their judgements, inspectors should consider the extent to which:

• one or more specified criteria are met.

SCHOOL DATA AND INDICATORS

PART C OF THE INSPECTION REPORT

After OTHER SPECIFIED FEATURES, if any, the inspection report will contain data and indicators which are defined by the report template that is in use at the time of the inspection.

THE INSPECTION OF OTHER FEATURES

The inspection focus for any additional features for inspection, for example a survey of an issue over a particular term, will be specified along with the feature itself.

Each feature specified will be accompanied by:

- an evaluation and reporting requirement indicated by ☐;

- up to three inspection criteria;

- a commentary covering the inspection focus;

- a summary of reporting requirements;

- guidance in the format of this *Handbook*, including sections on the inspection focus, making your judgement, and guidance on the inspection criteria.

10. THE STANDARDS AND QUALITY OF TEACHING IN AREAS OF THE CURRICULUM, SUBJECTS AND COURSES

FULL INSPECTIONS ONLY – PART D OF THE INSPECTION REPORT

Areas of learning (or the Foundation Curriculum for nursery and reception pupils)

The report must include evaluation of:

☐ the standards achieved, stating the extent to which pupils are on course to reach the expected outcomes or goals by 5 years and the quality of teaching in each area of learning;

☐ changes since the previous inspection;

☐ any other factors which have a bearing on what is achieved in the areas of learning.

The report should highlight any differences in provision or attainment for pupils who are 5 or under in nursery, reception or mixed-age classes.

Subjects and courses

For each subject or course, where evidence allows, the report should include evaluation of:

☐ how well pupils have achieved in the subject, particularly the standards achieved by the oldest pupils in each Key Stage, highlighting what pupils do well and could do better;

☐ changes since the previous inspection;

☐ how well pupils are taught, highlighting effective and ineffective teaching in the subjects and relating the demands made by teachers to pupils' learning and the progress they have made;

☐ any other factors which have a bearing on what is achieved, especially the extent to which management of this subject is directed towards monitoring, evaluating and improving performance.

In English and mathematics, the subject reports of work up to 16 should draw on evidence of the contribution made by other subjects to pupils' competence in literacy and numeracy respectively. In information and communications technology (ICT), the report should draw on evidence of contributions made to pupils' IT capability from all other subjects.

In schools with pupils of primary age, the report must include separate sections on English and mathematics. It should include sections on other subjects of the basic curriculum where there is sufficient evidence. In schools with pupils of secondary age, the report should include sections on all subjects of the basic curriculum up to and post-16, and any other courses or subjects included in the inspection contract. In schools having post-16 provision, the report should include a section on vocational courses and other post-16 provision. GNVQ or other vocational courses can be grouped together unless the inspection contract includes the inspection of specific component courses.

PART 2

GUIDANCE FOR INSPECTORS ON CONDUCTING INSPECTIONS AND WRITING REPORTS

INSPECTION QUALITY

1   This guidance will help you to interpret the inspection requirements set out in *Inspecting Schools*, the inspection Framework. It follows the sequence of work required before, during and after an inspection.

2   The guidance is for all inspectors and contractors. The registered inspector is ultimately responsible for the inspection and the report. This guidance therefore focuses particularly on his/her role. However, all inspectors in a team must work to the inspection requirements set out here, especially the Code of Conduct, and measure up to the Quality Guarantee for teachers. The inspection contractor has to meet OFSTED's Quality Assurance Standard as a condition for being awarded inspection work.

Setting a standard for inspection

3   As an inspector, you need to have high personal and professional qualities. When inspecting, you should treat all the people you meet – pupils, parents, staff, governors and others – as you would expect them to treat you, with interest, courtesy and respect. You should regard your right of entry to schools as a privilege.

4   Assessing the professional competence of others can arouse anxieties. Inspection is no exception. You must see to it that you recognise and praise strengths as well as probe areas of weakness. You must be alert to the sensitivities of staff but also be objective in all you do.

5   There are four main strands to inspection:

   ■ finding out what the school is like, and its strengths and weaknesses;

   ■ diagnosing what makes it the way it is;

   ■ identifying what it needs to do next to improve;

   ■ reflecting these findings back to the school, both orally and in the written inspection report.

6   Inspection is effective when it is seen by schools as fair, rigorous and helpful. The school must respect and value the quality and expertise of the inspection team. If it does, it will accept and make use of the inspection's findings to help it move forward. Otherwise, the usefulness of inspection is greatly reduced.

7   Inspection, therefore, must not only arrive at the right judgements but also be done in the right way.

Quality Guarantee for schools

8   We attach such a high priority to the effect of inspection on schools, that we expect all inspectors actively to reflect and promote the Quality Guarantee we give to teachers.

QUALITY GUARANTEE

- *Inspectors will do everything possible to work with you in keeping the stress of an inspection to a minimum.*

- *Inspectors will not expect you to create additional paperwork specifically for the inspection.*

- *Inspectors will always treat you in a courteous and friendly manner, particularly when entering and leaving your classroom.*

- *Normally, you will be observed teaching for no more than half of any one day, and never more than three-quarters.*

- *Inspectors will not judge teaching unless they have observed a significant part of the lesson, normally for at least 30 minutes.*

- *Inspectors will use confidential information responsibly.*

- *Inspectors will discuss important aspects of your teaching with you.*

- *Inspectors will explain the reasons for their judgements and be helpful in identifying where improvement is needed.*

---

9   Most inspectors reflect these principles naturally in their work. The great majority of the responses we receive from teachers and schools show that most inspectors have high standards of conduct and professionalism.

10   But there are exceptions. There is no place for inspectors who are remote from the teachers, brusque, overbearing in their behaviour, or insensitive. Nor should you ask the school for paperwork it does not normally use, such as lesson plans to a particular format.

OFSTED's expectations of inspectors

11   Our expectations of inspectors are set out in the Framework and include the following.

12   **You must be thoroughly prepared for the inspection and understand the context of the school and its pupils.** It takes time to prepare properly. You should ensure that the contractor gives you enough time. If you are a registered inspector, the quality of your *Pre-Inspection Commentary* is vital. If the issues it identifies are clear, and you brief your team well, the inspection will get off to a good start.

13   **You must have thorough knowledge and understanding of the Framework, this *Inspection Handbook*, the subjects and aspects you inspect and the age range of the pupils concerned.** You work in a changing educational scene. Curriculum requirements change, as do the national policies. You must keep yourself up to date. This means consulting documents from various sources: from OFSTED, the DfEE, the Qualifications and Curriculum Authority (QCA) and other relevant bodies. You need to have a thorough understanding of the special education needs for which the school (or unit) provides.

14 You must uphold the highest professional standards required by the Code of Conduct, thus securing OFSTED's Quality Guarantee to teachers *(see above)*.

CODE OF CONDUCT

15 The Code of Conduct has been revised. To meet its principles, you must:

■ **evaluate the work of the school objectively, be impartial and have no previous connection with the school, its staff or governors (or appropriate authority) which could undermine your objectivity;**

> We take the questions of impartiality and connection seriously. If you have had anything to do with the school in the past few years, you should consider carefully whether you should be part of the school's inspection team. You should certainly rule yourself out if this contact included any 'pre-inspection' work, staff appointments, advice or staff development. If in doubt, you should err on the side of caution. If you are a team inspector you must, as a condition of your enrolment, inform the registered inspector and contractor of any connection at all with the school.

■ **report honestly and fairly, ensuring that judgements accurately and reliably reflect what the school achieves and does;**

> Judgements must be robust and fully supported by evidence so that you can defend them, if required. They must be accurate and carefully weighed and tested against the inspection criteria. They must also be reliable, which means that other trained inspectors, using the same evidence, would be highly likely to come to the same judgement.

■ **carry out your work with integrity, treating all those you meet with courtesy and sensitivity;**

> It is important that you leave staff feeling as though they have been treated well and fairly.

■ **do all you can to minimise stress, in particular by ensuring that no teacher is over-inspected and by not asking for paperwork to be specifically prepared for the inspection;**

> We are committed to reducing stress among teachers as far as possible. Inspectors must do everything they can to allay anxiety. This must start from the moment they begin to have dealings with the school and continue until the report is published. Teachers are naturally apprehensive about inspection. We expect you to do what you can to put them at their ease. There are clear guidelines about how much teachers should be observed during a day. In special schools, all inspectors share the responsibility to ensure that these guidelines are followed.

■ **act with the best interests and well-being of pupils and staff as priorities;**

> The deal the pupils get is at the heart of your work. It is essential that you discover their views of the school as well as evaluating their educational progress and achievements. You must certainly not cause pupils any anxiety. You have many dealings with them during an inspection. Your questioning should not make them feel vulnerable or inadequate. Your relations with them must be a model of propriety. You must not put them in a position where they may feel conflicting loyalties.

■ **communicate with staff purposefully and productively, and present your judgements of the school's work clearly and frankly;**

> In your dealings with teachers and other staff, you should build confidence and mutual respect. You should seek to understand what they are doing and why, and share with them your views about what you find. We cannot stress enough the importance of feeding back your findings in a helpful way.

■ **respect the confidentiality of information, particularly about teachers and the judgements made about their individual teaching.**

> In judging teaching, you are undertaking a form of professional appraisal. You should not criticise the work of a teacher, or anyone else involved with the school, within earshot of someone else. You should relay concerns to the headteacher or appropriate manager, but not before discussing them with the teacher concerned. Do not allow yourself to be placed in a position where you cannot use information you are given in the way you think best. At times, you may need to make it clear that you reserve the right to do as you see fit with certain information or evidence.

THE RECORD OF INSPECTION EVIDENCE

16   The record of evidence comprises:

i.   forms completed by the school:

- *Form S1*, consultation with the appropriate authority about the specification for the inspection, and data about the school;

- *Form S2*, further data about the school;

- *Form S3*, school self-audit;

- *Form S4*, school monitoring and self-evaluation;

ii.   the *PANDA report* supplied by OFSTED to special schools;

iii. documentary evidence from the school (normally returned to the school after the inspection) and the previous inspection report;

iv.   evidence and judgements recorded by inspectors, including:

- *Pre-Inspection Commentary*, with issues for inspection;

- *Evidence Forms*;

- *Inspection Notebooks* – one is completed by each member of the team on FULL INSPECTIONS (optional in SHORT INSPECTIONS);

- the *Record of Corporate Judgements*;

- evidence from parents.

17   Further details of the record of evidence are given in the sections which follow. Instructions for their completion are summarised in Annex 3.

EFFICIENT AND EFFECTIVE INSPECTION

18   The process of inspection, like developing a photographic image, is the progressive unveiling of the school until its essential character can be seen. As each part of the picture is revealed the image becomes clearer. Because inspection is such a concentrated process, from the start it must use all the evidence available to hypothesise about the school's quality and standards, and its potential strengths and weaknesses. This gives a focus for the inspectors' work.

19   However, inspection is not a mere snapshot of a school. The quality and standards of each school in England are now documented in one or more previous inspection reports. Each school's performance has been measured, year after year. The school's own planning also reflects its changing priorities and needs. Each school has an ongoing record, showing where it has come from: a performance trail.

THE INSPECTION SEQUENCE

20   The registered inspector should take full account of the recent history of the school's quality and standards, particularly when gauging the extent of improvement.

21   You should also note what the school does to monitor and evaluate its own performance and what its evaluation shows. The inspection forms the school completes reflect the wish of many schools for inspectors to take self-evaluation into account.[1] *Form S3* invites the school to make its own assessment of compliance with statutory requirements: a self-audit. *Form S4* invites the school to present its own view of where it stands in relation to each of the areas of its work to be inspected. Using inspection to test the school's perceptions of itself gives an insight into how well it is managed. Inspection thus provides a mirror for the school. You should find out how the school sets individual targets and records progress.

22   The first stage of pre-inspection analysis should provide early hypotheses to follow up at the preliminary visit to the school. This visit should give you, as the registered inspector, a very helpful first impression of the *quality* of the school. It may be difficult for some headteachers to be available for discussion during the school day. By meeting the headteacher or teacher in charge, staff, governors or appropriate authority and pupils, and by looking round the school, you will get an important contextual picture to set alongside the data and documentary evidence.

23   You should now be in a position to complete most of the *Pre-Inspection Commentary* for the rest of the inspection team. Ideally this should take into account the views of parents, although this may depend on the timing of the parents' meeting. Your analysis must identify important issues and lines of enquiry for the inspection. Some of these may relate to apparent areas of strength or weakness, others to:

■   issues for action identified in the last inspection;

■   claims made by the school in its self-evaluation report;

---

[1]   This was also recommended by the Education and Employment Committee of the House of Commons, Fourth Report, *The Work of OFSTED*, London 1999.

- features that relate to the school's particular circumstances;
- areas identified by the headteacher for inspection.

Above all, the issues must be specific to the school.

24   *The Pre-Inspection Commentary* has three purposes. First, it forms the basis for briefing other members of the team so that they know a great deal about the school when they arrive to start the inspection. Secondly, it provides an agenda of inspection priorities. Thirdly, it contributes to the judgements for the inspection report.

25   As the inspection progresses, there is often a change in emphasis, from establishing what the standards are and how well they reflect the earlier data, to securing explanations of why the achievements of the school are as they are. The quality of teaching will be an early focus.

26   At the end of the inspection, there should be a clear and shared view among the whole inspection team of the overall quality and standards of the school. In other words, how good it is. You should evaluate against each of the main requirements of the inspection schedule, and the team should reach a consensus view on the school's strengths, any areas for improvement, and what the school needs to do to improve. This process is summarised below.

The inspection sequence

Before the inspection

During the inspection

At the end of the inspection

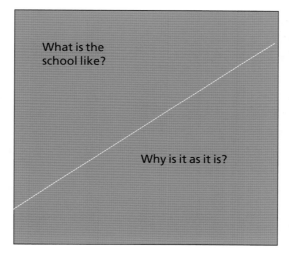
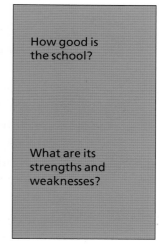

What does the school appear to be like?

Where should the inspection focus?

What is the school like?

Why is it as it is?

How good is the school?

What are its strengths and weaknesses?

Pre-inspection analysis provides an initial view of the standards and possible quality of the school, influenced by visiting the school and hearing the views of the parents.

Initial emphasis on verifying the standards of the school and evaluating the quality of its provision. As the inspection proceeds, the relative impact of different factors is assessed.

Inspectors agree their judgements about standards, quality, strengths and weaknesses, focusing on teaching, leadership and management.

Finally they identify what the school should do to improve.

BEFORE THE INSPECTION

NOTICE OF INSPECTION

27   OFSTED has reduced the notice of inspection given to schools to between six and ten school weeks. The purpose of this is to reduce the pressure on teachers and other staff, and to avoid long, drawn-out processes, such as rewriting documents and making other preparations which some schools have felt they needed to do. The shorter notice has been welcomed by most schools. However, it does put some pressure on the school to complete the inspection forms on time, and on the contractor and registered inspector to make the necessary arrangements for the inspection.

28   The shorter notice of inspection places a premium on efficient procedures in the run-up to inspection. The inspection will take place during a five-week 'inspection window'. The possible sequence of pre-inspection events is illustrated below. The first five steps are fixed by the 'inspection window'; the others will vary slightly in timing, depending on the date of the inspection.

Summary of pre-inspection steps

Six school weeks before the 'inspection window' (typically eight weeks before the inspection)	1. School receives notification of inspection, and whether this will be SHORT or FULL, and a set of inspection forms	
Five school weeks before the inspection window (typically seven weeks before the inspection)	2. School returns *Form S1* to OFSTED	3. Contractor receives specification from OFSTED with *Form S1* and sets date of inspection with school and registered inspector 4. Registered inspector contacts school
Two school weeks before the inspection window (typically four weeks before the inspection)		5. Contractor sends outline inspection plan to OFSTED and item list to OFSTED and the school
Four weeks before the inspection	6. School sends *Forms S2–S4*, plus previous inspection report, prospectus and development plan to registered inspector and calls meeting for parents	7. Registered inspector receives documents from school, and prepares for visit
Two or three weeks before the inspection		8. Registered inspector visits school 9. Registered inspector plans the inspection in detail
Two weeks before the inspection		10. Registered inspector meets parents 11. Registered inspector completes *Pre-Inspection Commentary*
Before the inspection begins		12. Registered inspector meets and briefs team

STEPS 1 AND 2: INSPECTION SPECIFICATION

29 As soon as the school is notified of the inspection and whether it is to be SHORT or FULL, it is asked to complete *Form S1* and return it to OFSTED within one week. At the same time, OFSTED supplies the school with *Forms S2, S3* and *S4*, which the school has three weeks to complete in electronic or hardcopy format.

30 *Form S1* allows the appropriate authority to provide basic information about the nature and composition of the school. *Form S1* is used to draw up the specification which OFSTED issues to the contractor as part of the contract for inspection; it will help the contractor to determine the composition of the inspection team.

STEP 3: SETTING THE DATE

31 Once it has the specification, the contractor should move immediately to let the school know who is to be the registered inspector, and to establish the date of the inspection with the school and the registered inspector.

STEP 4: COMMUNICATING WITH THE SCHOOL AND PARENTS

32 If you are the registered inspector for the inspection, you should make contact with the headteacher of the school and:

- introduce yourself;

- find out how the headteacher or teacher in charge, staff and governors or appropriate authority are viewing the forthcoming inspection;

- enquire about progress in completing the *Forms S2–S4* and arrange for them to be *sent to you*, together with the other prescribed documents (*see paragraph 34*);

- arrange a date and time to visit the school, explaining what you wish to do during the visit, and set up a programme for it;

- discuss and agree dates and times for other events, including the parents' meeting, feedback to senior management team and governing body or appropriate authority, the period over which the school can check the draft report, and the days the inspection will last;

- make the CVs of the inspection team available to the school.

STEPS 5, 6 AND 7: INITIAL PREPARATION

33 To make the most of your visit to the school you must prepare thoroughly. Contractors must make sure that time is provided for this.

34   You first need to assemble the core documents required before the visit. These are:

- *Form S1*, completed by the school and sent to you by OFSTED;

- *Forms S2, S3* and *S4* completed and sent to you by the school;

- the *PANDA report*;

- the last inspection report, provided by the school;

- the current school development or management plan, provided by the school;

- the school prospectus or brochure, provided by the school.

35   You must not require any other documents from the school at this stage. The school has enough to do in completing the four forms, calling the parents' meeting and communicating with governors. Remember that the inspection must do everything possible to avoid putting an extra burden on schools or significantly affecting their normal patterns of work.

36   Your analysis of indicators and documents should be systematic and your enquiries related to the questions posed in the inspection *Schedule*. WHAT SORT OF SCHOOL IS IT? is both the starting and the finishing point for your inspection. Start with the school's view of itself, expressed in its prospectus. Look at how it presents itself and what it considers to be important. Consider the extent to which pupils' interests are at the centre of the school's presentation and aspirations.

37   *Forms S1* and *S2* indicate who the pupils are, their background, mobility, home language and special educational needs. Look for evidence of effectiveness. Look at the pattern of the school's results from individual pupils' data, when available; trends over time; high and low spots; and comparative data, where appropriate. Look at other indications of effectiveness such as how the budget is constructed; the pattern of exclusions, if there are any; and attendance.

38   Then your analysis can move from outcomes to the quality of provision. Look at the curriculum as expressed qualitatively in the prospectus and quantitatively on *Form S2*. Consider whether it is giving the range of experiences you might expect, across the age range. Consider staffing and class organisation, the staff profile and deployment, and possible management issues. Look for the school's priorities for improvement reflected in the development plan.

39   After this analysis you should have a useful but partial picture of the school. This will include hypotheses that you will need to investigate further. What does this picture add up to? Where has the school come from and where is it heading? What appear to be the big issues in the school? What are the school's targets and is it likely to meet them? Two strong pieces of evidence are the previous inspection report and the headteacher's evaluation report on *Form S4*.

40   By putting the information from these different sources together, you should be able to: estimate how the school is performing; know what its priorities now are; see whether these have changed since the last inspection; and consider how the school views its own quality and standards. You will have an initial impression of the school which will form the basis for discussion when you meet the headteacher.

41   You are now in a position to begin to write the *Pre-Inspection Commentary*, which you will add to significantly and complete after the preliminary visit to the school. You should include views about:

- standards attained in the core subjects of English, mathematics and science, highlighting any patterns of strengths or weaknesses, where results of examinations are available;

- any trends in attainment over time, where appropriate;

- how these results compare to the last inspection;

- any significant change to the profile of pupils' attainment on entry;

- areas that might need further exploration during the inspection;

- the quality of management.

STEP 8: VISITING THE SCHOOL

42   The visit to the school is a very important part of the inspection process and is likely to last for a day. It has five main purposes:

i.   to establish a good and trusting working relationship between you (the registered inspector) and the school, particularly the headteacher or teacher in charge;

ii.   to gain a better understanding of the school, its nature, what it is aiming to do and how it goes about its work;

iii.   to consider aspects of the school on which inspectors might focus, some of which may be identified by the school;

iv.   to brief the staff and any governors or members of the appropriate authority who are able to meet you on how the inspection will work;

v.   to agree the necessary arrangements for the inspection.

43   To achieve these intentions you will need to plan the visit carefully, in consultation with the school.

44   Ideally, you will need to do the following during the initial visit:

- have an extensive discussion with the headteacher to find out more about the school and the way it is run, and to test your initial perceptions; and tour the school, to become acquainted with its geography, if possible meeting some pupils and staff;

- find out how the school sets targets and keeps its records of pupils' progress;

- agree a representative sample of pupils whose records will be analysed during the inspection;

- meet the staff of the school, to brief them on how the inspection will be organised and respond to any queries they may have;

- meet any representatives of the appropriate authority, again to discuss the inspection with them, but also to learn how it has been involved with developments since the last inspection, and how it perceives its current role and priorities. You should arrange to meet members during the inspection as well.

45 Your meetings with the headteacher, staff and the appropriate authority should put them at their ease by explaining how the inspection will be run, and give them confidence in the process. They should be helped to see how they can gain value from it. You should explain:

For a SHORT INSPECTION

■ how the SHORT INSPECTION can only be a light 'health check' of the school, not an intensive subject-by-subject inspection;

■ the basis for sampling lessons, with the possibility that some teachers or subjects will not be seen;

■ that inspectors will discuss work with teachers as they go, giving whatever feedback they can;

■ that the report will focus on the main strengths of the school and areas needing improvement.

For a FULL INSPECTION

■ that a significant amount of the work in every subject will be seen, though individual teachers may be observed on only one or two occasions;

■ how all teachers will be offered feedback on their work and receive their profile of lesson grades.

46 Discuss with the headteacher or teacher in charge the arrangements for the parents' meeting. Discuss whether the school can provide a room for the inspection team to work in during the inspection. If the school is unable to do this without disturbing its own work, the inspectors will have to make their own arrangements for a base.

47 During the preliminary visit, you should request from the school any additional documents which will be needed in advance of the inspection. These must be those which the school already has, or can easily supply. You should not ask the headteacher/teacher in charge to prepare additional documents specifically for the inspection. To make the inspection run smoothly, you will need:

■ a programme, or timetable, of the school's work in the period of the inspection;

■ a staff handbook, if one is available, or list of staff responsibilities and/or objectives;

■ a plan of the school.

48 In a FULL INSPECTION, you will need to take away, or see at a later stage, further documents such as:

■ the governors' annual report to parents, where applicable;

■ minutes of the meetings of the governing body, or the equivalent where the appropriate authority is not the governing body;

■ evidence of progress towards the targets set by the appropriate authority, where applicable;

■ curriculum plans, policies, guidelines or schemes of work already in existence;

■ the outcomes of self-evaluations carried out recently by the school;

■ the outcomes of any external monitoring and evaluations carried out since the last inspection;

■ any other documentation the school wishes you to consider, subject to your agreement.

You should return all of these to the school after the inspection.

49   In a SHORT INSPECTION, you should avoid taking further documentation away from the school. You should not ask the school to collect together curriculum plans, policies, guidelines or schemes of work, no matter how important the school feels they are. Only if specific issues arise during the inspection, where the reasons for a particular strength or weakness need be explored, should you ask to see any related material.

50   There is a lot of ground to cover on the preliminary visit; therefore it is not ideal to hold the parents' meeting on the same day.

STEP 9: PLANNING THE INSPECTION

51   The registered inspector should:

- ensure responsibilities are assigned for all subjects and aspects, equal opportunities; and, where relevant, the post-16 provision and English as an additional language;

- decide the deployment of the team on the basis of a clear strategy for sampling the work of the school, taking account of the areas of expertise of team members;

- plan the deployment of inspectors, particularly on the first day, and ensure that each inspector has an appropriate schedule of inspection activities to cover in addition to his/her responsibilities;

- plan to collect evidence relating to particular aspects identified as focal points in the *Pre-Inspection Commentary*;

- plan, in conjunction with the school, when discussions with staff will take place and, on FULL INSPECTIONS, agree when the feedback to subject co-ordinators and classroom teachers will be held;

- in SHORT INSPECTIONS, decide whether or not *Inspection Notebooks* will be used;

- set deadlines for team inspectors to complete *Inspection Notebooks* (remember that, apart from the draft sections for the report, these must be completed before the final team meeting);

- in FULL INSPECTIONS, set deadlines for team inspectors to submit draft sections for the report.

STEP 10: MEETING WITH PARENTS

52   The pre-inspection meeting with parents is a legal requirement. The meeting must take place before the inspection begins so that the registered inspector can fully consider the parents' views as important pre-inspection evidence. Parents should have as much notice of the meeting as possible. The 'appropriate authority' (usually the governing body) is responsible for organising the meeting. Only parents of pupils registered at the school should be invited. The headteacher or a member of the appropriate authority may introduce you to the parents at the meeting. Any member of staff, or governor, who is also a parent of a pupil at the school may attend the meeting. OFSTED provides a sample letter of invitation and the suggested agenda for the meeting (available on the CD-ROM attached to this *Handbook*).

53   The registered inspector should invite the appropriate authority to distribute the standard questionnaire to parents (available on the CD-ROM). Individual responses are confidential to the inspection team and there should be arrangements to ensure that this is the case. Inspection contractors have translations of the questionnaire in the more commonly used home languages and at an early stage you should check with the school whether these are needed. If forms in other languages are used, you will need to plan to have comments translated.

54   The school should distribute the questionnaire on the basis of one per pupil. However, its normal procedures should be used where information is sent separately to more than one person with responsibility for the child, making sure that sufficient questionnaires are sent so that parents can respond separately for each child.

55   You should base the meeting on the standard agenda for parents' meetings (available on the CD-ROM) and give parents the opportunity to express their views on:

- the standards the school achieves;

- how the school helps pupils, whatever their ability, to learn and make progress;

- the attitudes and values the school promotes;

- behaviour and attendance;

- the work the school expects pupils to do at home; and the school's links with parents, including information on how pupils are getting on;

- how the school responds to parents' suggestions and concerns;

- how the school has improved in recent years.

56   You should also invite views on any other matters which the parents may wish to raise. You should ask parents not to name individual pupils and teachers at any stage during the meeting. You should explain in general terms the forthcoming inspection and its purpose. You may need to explain why the school has been selected for a particular type of inspection.

57   As soon as possible after the meeting is over, and you have received the returned questionnaires and analysed them, you should discuss with the headteacher/teacher in charge the significant issues and concerns raised by parents. You should give him or her the opportunity to offer you other evidence of parents' views about the school. You should explain that the inspectors' views on what parents say about the school will form part of the feedback at the end of the inspection, and also will be contained in the written report.

STEP 11: COMPLETION OF THE *PRE-INSPECTION COMMENTARY*

58   After the visit to the school, you should be in a position to prepare a detailed, well-informed and penetrating *Pre-Inspection Commentary* on the school. This commentary should be completed for as many sections of the schedule as possible.

59   You should give preliminary views about:

- the characteristics of the school;

- any evidence of trends in attainment, and improvement since the last inspection, adding to your existing commentary on these areas;

- attendance and exclusions, with potential views on attitudes and behaviour;

- the match of staff expertise to subjects taught and any implications for attainment shown in the data;

- the range and quality of the school's educational provision and other aspects of the school, making full use of the school's documents provided.

60   You should present initial hypotheses about the school's provisions and its possible impact on pupils' progress. These might include:

- possible changes in the quality of teaching caused by staff turnover, monitoring and evaluation strategies, or in-service training;

- features of the school's context and organisation, such as changes to admissions criteria;

- the impact of the school's context and its leadership and management;

- changes in curriculum provision, such as the introduction of accredited courses;

- the use of resources to promote standards.

61   These are matters that you must pursue in the inspection. You should also form hypotheses about:

- the extent, and adequacy, of the school's improvement since the last inspection;

- whether the school might be underachieving, has serious weaknesses, or requires special measures.

62   In considering the pre-inspection information, do not lose sight of the wood for the trees. Ensure that the *Pre-Inspection Commentary* paints the 'big picture' of the school, and that the central hypotheses about the school stand out clearly. Effective *Pre-Inspection Commentaries* for both SHORT and FULL INSPECTIONS:

- draw on the full range of pre-inspection evidence, including the school's self-evaluation, views formed during the pre-inspection visit, parents' views and returned questionnaires;

- build substantially on the issues raised in the previous inspection report; and the school's actions in response to them;

- where possible provide an accurate historical analysis of the school's achievements and trends;

- identify hypotheses for further exploration or confirmation: issues for inspection.

STEP 12: TEAM BRIEFING AND MEETING

63　The team should meet for a final briefing before starting the inspection. You should note that:

- this is more than a short gathering before the first morning's inspection begins. A thorough briefing is required;

- it could be a morning meeting prior to beginning the inspection in the afternoon, or a separate meeting before the first day of the inspection;

- the meeting must not encroach on inspection time;

- the meeting should be for the whole inspection team, and where any team member begins the inspection at a later stage, arrangements must be made for a thorough briefing at that stage.

64　As the registered inspector, you will check the background and strengths of the team, if you do not already know them, and then:

- brief the team about the school and the *Pre-Inspection Commentary*;

- alert the team to any concerns or anxieties felt by the school or staff;

- ensure that all members of the team gather evidence against all the schedule headings;

- ensure that all members of the team know exactly what their first day's programme is to be;

- on FULL INSPECTIONS, ensure they have completed their subject *Pre-Inspection Commentaries*;

- clarify organisation and administrative arrangements;

- ensure that all are clear about their expected conduct.

65　You should make sure that the team is aware of all the issues and how these are to be tracked through. But above all, inspectors need to be aware of the 'big issues'. For example, if there is a strong boy/girl difference in achievements, this should be clearly stated so that inspectors reflect their relative performance in each *Evidence Form* they write. The team should understand the school almost as well as you do by the end of the briefing.

THE ROLE OF THE REGISTERED INSPECTOR

66   As the registered inspector, you are the manager of the inspection team and the whole inspection process, and the first point of reference for everyone involved in the inspection. Effective management and organisation of the team on a day-to-day basis are crucial to the success of the inspection. It is your responsibility to ensure that judgements about the school are fair and accurate, are based on secure and representative evidence, comprehensively cover the schedule and contract requirements, and are corporately agreed. You are responsible for drawing key judgements together in the *Record of Corporate Judgements*.

67   You should:

- ensure that inspectors are consistent in their approaches to collecting and recording evidence and in how they conduct themselves and provide feedback to teachers;

- be prepared to adjust the patterns of work of individual inspectors as circumstances dictate;

- monitor and, if necessary, intervene in the work of the team to ensure compliance with the Framework and secure the necessary quality of evidence and judgements;

- undertake direct inspection such as observing work in classrooms, sampling pupils' records, and holding discussions with staff, governors or members of the appropriate authority and pupils;

- keep a careful check on the sampling of the school's work and the extent of observation of individual teachers.

TEAM INSPECTORS' ASSIGNMENTS

68   Inspectors need to plan and use their time carefully and efficiently to achieve the coverage required, but they should be sensitive to the impact of the inspection on teachers and other staff in the school. Inspecting and evaluating the following aspects of the school's work will require contributions from the whole team but will need to be co-ordinated by one inspector:

- equality of opportunity for different groups of pupils;

- pupils' spiritual, moral, social and cultural development.

69   In FULL INSPECTIONS, inspectors need to draw evidence relating to their subject from across the curriculum. So, for example, the inspector leading on the inspection of English will need to take account of pupils' literacy skills and opportunities for developing these competencies in subjects other than English. This will require other inspectors to contribute. The same is true for mathematics, in relation to numeracy skills, and information technology. In these cases, the inspector taking the lead will need evidence from across the curriculum.

70   Team meetings are an essential part of any inspection. They allow contributions from all inspectors and generate a sense of common purpose based on good working relationships, and a clear understanding of everyone's responsibilities within the team. As the registered inspector, you should structure and manage these meetings to provide opportunities for:

- the proper consideration and exchange of inspection evidence and inspectors' views;

- discussion of emerging issues which require the attention of the whole team;

- the resolution of issues for inspection identified in the *Pre-Inspection Commentary*;

- discussion of any gaps or weaknesses in the evidence base and how to fill them;

- debate about evidence, views and judgements to ensure consistency and to resolve any conflicts where they arise.

71   It is good practice to establish a programme of team meetings with clear agendas before the inspection begins. You will need to build in some flexibility to take account of any emerging issues during the inspection. Team meetings must not encroach on inspection time.

GATHERING THE INSPECTION EVIDENCE

72   Within their assignments on FULL INSPECTIONS, individual inspectors must be allocated time to collect evidence on all parts of the *Evaluation Schedule*, so that they can contribute to the team's corporate judgements. They must also ensure they have enough evidence to form judgements in their own subjects. The evidence includes:

- the inspection of teaching and of pupils at work in classrooms and other areas; and work off-site where the inspection priorities allow, where there is agreement with the 'appropriate authority', and where it is practicable and manageable;

- the inspection of teaching on courses in other schools where they are dual registered, where this is significant;

- discussions with pupils, for example, to assess their understanding and knowledge of different subjects and their attitudes to work and their life at school;

- the analysis of samples of pupils' work within individual subjects and across the curriculum;

- discussions with staff, especially those with management responsibilities, such as heads of department and heads of year;

- documentary analysis of schemes of work and teachers' plans, together with records of National Curriculum tests and teachers' assessments, any assessment undertaken of attainment on entry and, where appropriate, examination results, and other measures or indicators of attainment and progress used by the school;

- the analysis of statements of special educational needs, annual and transitional reviews and individual education plans.

73   The evidence should be recorded on *Evidence Forms* and summarised in *Inspection Notebooks* as the inspection proceeds.

74   In SHORT INSPECTIONS, **all** inspectors will collect evidence, mainly from observation of lessons, across all relevant parts of the *Evaluation Schedule*. Individual inspectors will be assigned during the inspection to follow up particular issues, often through discussions, and will need to report these back to the rest of the team at team meetings. You should try to avoid undertaking too much documentary analysis in a SHORT INSPECTION. Confine this to those areas where there are particular strengths or weaknesses, to follow up why things are the way they are. The evidence should be recorded on *Evidence Forms*. If you choose to do so, you can use *Inspection Notebooks* to help you record your views and judgements and to structure your contribution to team meetings.

OBSERVATION OF LESSONS AND OTHER ACTIVITIES

75   While the school is in session the inspection team should aim to spend at least 60 per cent of its time observing lessons and sampling pupils' work and records. The time spent in lessons will vary, but some whole lessons must be observed. Lessons or sessions observed should be from the school's normal programme of work. Inspectors should not require changes to that programme.

76   In SHORT INSPECTIONS the sample of lessons should provide a cross-section of the work of the school. You should focus on the beginnings and ends of Key Stages and at the end of courses in post-16 provision. You should select the sample to include observation of the teaching of those teachers who hold management and/or curricular responsibility, for example:

■ the headteacher/teacher in charge if he/she is in charge of a class or has a significant teaching load;

■ the deputy headteacher;

■ English, mathematics and personal social and health education co-ordinators teaching their subject (or a literacy hour, for example);

■ those responsible for the early years and Key Stages and post-16 students.

77   In FULL INSPECTIONS lesson observations should include sufficient work in each Key Stage. Inspectors should spend enough time in lessons to enable them to make valid and reliable judgements on standards, teaching and learning. There should be a particular focus on the attainment of the oldest pupils. You must aim to observe each teacher present in the school during the inspection at least once.

78   In nursery classes or units with nursery-aged children or classes, you should observe the oldest and youngest children, recording your evidence for these groups on separate *Evidence Forms*. In mixed-age classes you should, as far as possible, also record the evidence for different age groups on separate forms. You should ensure that adequate time is allowed to inspect the full range of subjects taught in post-16 provision.

79   Small schools serving pupils with a wide age range face particular challenges and you will need to evaluate how well they are met. For example:

• the class(es) cater for a wide age range	• raises questions about the match of work and providing appropriate challenges and resources for all, particularly if pupils are in different Key Stages
• pupils may remain in one class for three, four or more years	• raises questions about whether the curriculum is planned to cover several years, avoiding repetition and retaining freshness, breadth and progression
• teaching staff, on the whole, may lack expertise in one or more curriculum areas	• raises questions about how the school redresses this
• pupils, particularly at the ends of Key Stages, may have few peers of the same age or capability	• raises questions about whether the school makes any arrangements to compensate for social and intellectual isolation
• there may only be a few nursery-aged children for certain days of the week	• raises the question of how appropriate are the school's curriculum, equipment and spaces for young children

80   Effective inspection involves looking at the work of individual pupils and discussing it with them. It also entails careful observation of teaching, including the organisation of work for pupils as a class, in groups or individually. Both need to be done so as not to disrupt either teaching or learning, and the taking of notes should be as unobtrusive as possible.

81   The load on teachers should be spread as evenly as possible. Wherever possible, teachers should not be kept waiting for their first visit from an inspector until near the end of the inspection. Inspectors should visit classes taught by supply teachers who are in the school for more than one day, and trainee teachers.

82   There should not normally be more than one inspector in a class at any time unless the class teacher agrees and there is a particular reason for it. An example would be to track the progress of a pupil with additional special educational needs, or where the registered inspector monitors the work of team members.

83   Inspection should include assemblies, extra-curricular activities, including sport if offered, and registration periods. It may also include fieldwork and educational visits where justifiable and practicable.

TALKING WITH PUPILS

84   Talking to pupils is a good source of evidence about what they know, can do and understand. It is particularly helpful in judging the extent of their understanding of current and recent work, and their ability to apply knowledge in different contexts. These discussions should take place as inspectors join individual pupils or groups of pupils at work in lessons. You should also use every opportunity to talk to pupils outside lessons, to find out their views of the school, their attitudes, their interests and the extent to which these are supported or fulfilled.

85   In all observation, it is important to listen to pupils':

- incidental talk and comments;

- contributions in class;

- responses to questions;

- questions, initiated by them;

- views, feelings and comments expressed in discussions.

THE ANALYSIS OF PUPILS' WORK

86   Pupils' earlier and current work provides an essential source of evidence of their attainment and progress. It also offers an insight into the curriculum, teaching and pupils' attitudes to work. You will need to look at samples of work and pupils' records of progress made. The nature of the samples should be agreed with the headteacher during the preliminary visit.

87   It is helpful if the analysis takes place near the beginning of the inspection in order to establish the team's view about the progress made by pupils, focusing on English, mathematics and personal, social and health education (PSHE).

88   In SHORT INSPECTIONS the sample should include the work and records of the oldest pupils in English, mathematics and PSHE.

89   In FULL INSPECTIONS, the sample should include the work and records of as many pupils as possible throughout the school.

90   For each pupil, targets set over a period of at least 12 months, should be available in order to establish the range of work covered over time and to evaluate evidence of progress. Inspectors will find it helpful to have pupils' records available alongside other evidence, such as video or audio records of attainment, with details of individual planning set at annual reviews and copies of statements.

DISCUSSION WITH STAFF, THE 'APPROPRIATE AUTHORITY' AND OTHERS INVOLVED IN THE WORK OF THE SCHOOL

91   Headteachers and registered inspectors alike value a daily meeting to agree administrative details, discuss any matters of concern, clarify inspection issues and obtain further information. These meetings contribute a great deal to the smooth running of an inspection and the maintenance of good relationships by sharing emerging hypotheses, providing the opportunity for the school to offer further evidence, and preparing the way for some of the judgements made at the end of the inspection.

92   Discussions with the headteacher, representatives of the 'appropriate authority', staff with particular management responsibilities and subject teachers provide important sources of evidence relating to roles and responsibilities, procedures and policies. They are essential to the professional dialogue between staff and inspectors, which contributes to the usefulness of inspection to schools. These discussions also help inspectors establish the context for their observations.

93   Discussion with teachers, especially at the end of lessons or sessions, is desirable, but it may not always be possible to have more than a brief exchange. However, the work of teachers should be acknowledged and as many opportunities as possible found for professional dialogue. Such dialogue might involve clarifying the context of the lesson or session, and of future work, as well as providing a brief evaluation of the quality of work seen, where this is possible. In SHORT INSPECTIONS the discussion at the end of, or shortly after, the lesson should provide brief feedback whenever possible on the quality of the teaching observed and any significant strengths and weaknesses.

94   You should arrange to meet staff and representatives of the 'appropriate authority' to discuss their areas of responsibility at mutually convenient times. This is best arranged by negotiation before the inspection starts. Where possible you should indicate the points you wish to raise in the discussion, giving those concerned time to think about the issues. You should not offer a pro forma which teachers may feel under extra pressure to prepare for and complete. Take care that meetings do not make unreasonable demands on teachers' time, for instance their break times. To ensure efficient use of teachers' and inspectors' time, you should plan and co-ordinate carefully the meetings with staff who have several responsibilities. Discussions with support staff, voluntary helpers and any visiting specialists, for example speech therapists, are also a valuable source of information and contribute to involving all staff in a FULL INSPECTION. It will not be possible to do this to the same extent on a SHORT INSPECTION.

THE PLACE OF DOCUMENTARY EVIDENCE

95 Schools should be judged primarily by their achievements, and on the effectiveness of their teaching, leadership and management in contributing to pupils' progress. Where a school is very effective, there is little need to trawl through all its procedural documents.

96 In the past, schools have spent an inordinate amount of time in preparing policies and revising curriculum plans or schemes, largely because of a forthcoming inspection. We wish to discourage this practice. Special schools are required by regulations to have a number of procedures and policies; other policies are simply recommended or encouraged by the DfEE or other national organisations. The presence or absence of non-statutory policies or documents is not intrinsically material to the quality and standards of the school. For example, a school is unremarkable if it achieves good attendance in a situation where you would expect attendance to be good. Where attendance is surprisingly good or is unsatisfactory, then you should investigate either why the school has achieved such unusually high attendance or, conversely, the reasons for attendance being poor and what the school is doing or has done about it. In either of these cases, it is appropriate to look into the school's policy and procedures in respect of attendance, the way it handles absence, the dealings it has with parents over the question of attendance, and so on. A school should not be marked down simply for not having an attendance policy, unless the absence of such a policy, for example in a school with poor attendance, indicates a measure of complacency in dealing with the issue.

97 In all inspections, schools are asked to complete a school self-audit (*Form S3*). The school is not expected to undertake extensive audit activities in order to do this; it would normally be sufficiently well informed about what is required and how it meets those requirements. The form illustrates a range of areas in which statutory requirements apply to all or some schools. You should know what these requirements are.

98 In a SHORT INSPECTION, the small scale of the inspection means that only if a concern is raised during the inspection will the inspection team explore the school's compliance with the detail of statutory requirements. In a FULL INSPECTION, however, one or more inspectors from the team should follow up the school's compliance in a range of areas as part of, and relevant to, their responsibilities.

99 In a SHORT INSPECTION, inspectors should sample the planning which underpins some of the lessons they see, but should not *unless there is a significant concern* call for and inspect all the school's plans or schemes of work for different subjects. Nor should they ask for policy or operational documents unless they are material to the investigation of particular strengths and weaknesses.

100 In a FULL INSPECTION, inspectors should not require a school to produce voluminous documentation in advance of the inspection. They should look at the plans or schemes for the subjects they are inspecting as they exist in the school, either before or at an early stage in the inspection. The burden on schools of writing or photocopying must be kept to an *absolute* minimum, and schools should be reimbursed for any copying costs.

DISCUSSING YOUR FINDINGS WITH TEACHERS AND OTHER PARTIES

101 How well the messages given during feedback are received and acted upon depends much on the trust, respect and rapport established between you and the headteacher and staff during the inspection. The way you communicate findings is also important. You should therefore:

- **gain teachers' acceptance;**

  This includes talking with the teachers and other staff about their work as the inspection develops, showing sensitivity in your dealings with them and their pupils as evidence is collected, and interacting with the pupils as much as possible – though discreetly – during lesson observations.

- **consider the effects of non-verbal as well as verbal messages during feedback and at other times.**

  Eye contact and appropriate facial expression, posture, gesture, voice, pace and tone can all help to reduce anxiety, gain acceptance of inspection findings and encourage constructive professional dialogue. Oral messages and body language should always be compatible.

102 You should offer feedback to every teacher observed. The objective is to help improve the teacher's effectiveness. Whenever possible, you should give firsthand feedback on the lessons you have observed. The purpose is to let teachers know your perception of the quality of the lessons and responses of pupils: what went well; what was less successful; and what could be done more effectively. Feedback should therefore:

- **identify the most important strengths and weaknesses in the teaching observed;**

  You must be selective in what you say and not simply rehearse everything that you have seen. Illustrate general conclusions with specific and practical examples from the evidence you have. You should not strive to find weaknesses in teaching that has none.

- **provide clear reasons for what you judged to be successful or otherwise;**

  Strengths and weaknesses should always be linked to their effects on pupils' learning, and must be attributed to the teaching approaches used rather than the teacher.

- **identify points for development.**

  Where the teaching is less than satisfactory, you should diagnose precisely what is not working and spell out what is needed to bring about improvement. It is equally important to identify how satisfactory and good teaching can be improved. You should, of course, acknowledge very good teaching and the features that make it so, but even here it is helpful if more subtle improvements can be identified.

FEEDBACK ON LESSONS

103   Where teaching is effective, feedback can usually be managed successfully after lessons – either at the end of the lesson if this is possible, or at a later time during the day, if this is more convenient. Where there are concerns, you may need time to reflect upon what you have seen and, more particularly, upon how you might best discuss your findings with the teacher concerned. It is helpful to see more than one lesson before feeding back about unsatisfactory teaching, to gauge whether weaknesses are sustained.

104   In a SHORT INSPECTION, the team is unlikely to be able to see a sufficient sample of the work of all teachers to give a view of the overall quality of their teaching. Some will not be seen teaching; others may only be visited for a single lesson. In very effective schools, one expects to see few, if any, weaknesses in the teaching. You are not required to provide summary feedback to teachers towards or at the end of the inspection but you should give whatever feedback you can as you go along. In SHORT INSPECTIONS, teachers will not be given a profile of the judgements on their teaching.

105   In a FULL INSPECTION, you should offer teachers summary feedback on the teaching that has been observed. Towards the end of the inspection, strengths and weaknesses in what has been seen can be pulled together. (More than one inspector may have seen the work of an individual teacher.) So the summary feedback to each teacher at the end of the inspection needs to be carefully co-ordinated to ensure that the inspector responsible for the feedback is well informed. Wherever possible, the inspector who is assigned to give feedback to a particular teacher should be the one who is best placed, by virtue of expertise or firsthand evidence collected, to make the greatest contribution to the professional development of that teacher. At the end of the inspection, each teacher is given a written record of the inspectors' judgements of their teaching, with a copy to the headteacher.

106   The requirement for individual performance feedback applies to:

■ full-time and part-time teachers;

■ supply teachers, except those working for less than five days in the school;

■ teachers funded under Ethnic Minorities Achievement Grant (EMAG) and other grants for specific purposes;

■ others, such as qualified support teachers, where they are responsible for classes or groups of children or the focus of evaluation of teaching has been on their work.

107   The requirement to provide individual performance feedback does not apply to the following staff and helpers, although you should offer it where possible. These staff are not given the written profile of judgements about their teaching, where their work was the focus of observation. However, you should include as many of these people as possible in ongoing dialogue about their work and contribution. Their recorded work will be collated under a composite heading OTHER CONTRIBUTIONS TO TEACHING in the profile given to the headteacher. The profiles of teaching judgements is not given to:

■ trainee teachers;

■ nursery and other classroom assistants;

■ special needs support assistants;

■ speech, physio- or occupational therapists;

- non-teaching support assistants;

- artists and writers in residence;

- instructors and coaches;

- visitors and other voluntary helpers.

FEEDBACK TO HEADS OF DEPARTMENTS/SUBJECT OR PHASE CO-ORDINATORS

108   Feedback to those with management responsibility for subjects or key aspects of the school's work is essential. Usually there is 'drip-feeding' of evaluations and sharing of hypotheses during the inspection, and summary feedback at the end of the week. There should be no major surprises at the end of the inspection. The summary feedback should:

- present the significant inspection findings supported by sufficient evidence so that the reasons for judgements are understood;

- provide an opportunity to clarify the findings;

- explore areas of disagreement;

- examine priorities for action;

- give the heads of departments, subject or phase co-ordinators a clear basis on which to start planning for improvement.

109   In a SHORT INSPECTION, you are unlikely to see a large enough sample of work to come to unequivocal views of quality and standards in all the subjects of the curriculum. In these circumstances, and taking account of the brevity of the inspection, you are not required to offer feedback to subject or phase heads of departments or co-ordinators at the end of the inspection. It is enough to do what you can as you go along.

110   In a FULL INSPECTION, feedback should be given to as many heads of departments or subject co-ordinators as possible. It should give them a clear picture of the inspection findings in their subject. In particular, it should rehearse the significant evidence and judgements about:

- standards in the subject;

- the quality of teaching and learning in the subject;

- improvement since the last inspection;

- areas identified as particular strengths and weaknesses;

- issues identified by inspection as priorities for improving the school.

THE FINAL TEAM MEETING

111   The main purpose of this team meeting is to arrive at accurate and thoroughly secure corporate judgements about the school, recording these in the *Record of Corporate Judgements*. You, as the registered inspector, need to manage this meeting so that the hypotheses tested out during the inspection are discussed and conclusions reached. You need to bring judgements together so that the culmination of the meeting is the team's overall view of the effectiveness of the school. The strengths and weaknesses recorded in WHAT THE SCHOOL DOES WELL and WHAT COULD BE IMPROVED also need to be specifically agreed by the team.

112   Therefore, all inspectors need to have reflected on their evidence in reaching their own views, and to be prepared to contribute these at the meeting. This means the meeting must not take place immediately after the inspection finishes. If the inspection finishes at lunchtime, you will need time to complete your *Inspection Notebook* in a FULL INSPECTION, or to gather your thoughts together in a SHORT INSPECTION before a meeting later in the afternoon. If the inspection finishes at the end of the school day, the final team meeting must not be held that day.

113   The meeting must be structured to achieve the goals set out above. In particular, the following areas must be included:

- discussions leading to the completion of the *Record of Corporate Judgements*;

- agreement about the contents of the summary of the inspection report;

- considering, as a team, whether the school is in need of special measures, has serious weaknesses or is underachieving.

114   We expect that all inspectors will attend this team meeting. We recognise that there will be exceptional circumstances where this is not possible. If that is the case, the inspector concerned must provide the registered inspector with his/her completed *Inspection Notebook* (except the draft text for the report) and any additional points that need to be brought to the attention of other inspectors.

FEEDBACK TO THE HEADTEACHER/TEACHER IN CHARGE AND SENIOR STAFF

115   Your feedback should give senior management an early but firm basis on which to start planning in response to the inspection's findings. In particular, the feedback to senior management should rehearse the significant evidence and judgements about:

- the school's outcomes, particularly standards achieved by pupils;

- the factors which most account for what is achieved, particularly the strengths and weaknesses in teaching in the school;

- the effectiveness of work done by managers and heads of departments/or subject co-ordinators;

- the issues identified by inspection as priorities for improving the school.

116　The staff attending the meeting should have the opportunity to clarify any of these findings, ask for further examples of evidence on which particular judgements about the school are based, and explore with inspectors the priorities for action.

117　The feedback to the headteacher and invited staff must be after the inspection has finished. It must not be on the last day of the inspection or even the day after. As the registered inspector, you must leave sufficient time to reflect on the evidence and corporate judgements in order to prepare properly.

118　The headteacher can invite whom he or she wishes to the feedback meeting, but it is usually for the senior management team only. No one other than the staff of the school should normally attend. There may be exceptional circumstances when the presence of an LEA officer as an observer is justified, for example:

- if the school has a temporary headteacher pending a permanent appointment;

- if the headteacher is judged likely to find the inspection findings distressing.

119　In such exceptional circumstances, the school can invite the officer only with the consent of the registered inspector.

120　The formal feedback should not be confused with the interim feedback offered to headteachers towards the end of an inspection by many registered inspectors. This is helpful to the school in relieving uncertainties and stress.

FEEDBACK TO THE 'APPROPRIATE AUTHORITY'

121　The success of the feedback to the 'appropriate authority', usually the governing body, hinges on how effectively inspectors communicate the main inspection findings clearly and frankly to a mixed audience, many of whom are well-informed but not professional teachers or educators. The same general principles apply to giving feedback to the governing body as to the senior management team, but the presentation to the governing body should have much less detail. The presentation should include a careful explanation of specific matters which should be included in the post-inspection plan. This is to ensure that the governing body is clear at an early stage about what the school should do to improve. It will often help to use visual aids to summarise the main points of the presentation.

122　The governing body for an LEA-maintained school may, if it wishes, invite an LEA officer (or diocesan education officer or similar religious adviser in the case of schools with a religious character) to be present as an observer at the oral feedback to the governing body. In most cases you will wish to include these observers in the dialogue. However, as the registered inspector, you may need to remind observers of their role if they become too assertive.

SOME GENERAL POINTS ABOUT FEEDBACK

123   Formal feedback meetings must take place before the inspection report is finished and as soon as is practicable after the inspection. The content of the oral feedback is confidential and the findings of the inspection should not be released, particularly to parents and the press, until after the 'appropriate authority' has received the inspection report. You may wish to remind those attending these meetings of their confidentiality.

124   The quality of the feedback is an important factor in influencing how the school responds to the inspection findings, and particularly in drawing up its post-inspection action plan for improvement. Effective feedback:

- is well structured, clear, succinct and unrushed;

- makes use of appropriate visual aids to help communicate the inspection findings, especially to governing bodies;

- places greater emphasis on what the school does well and what could be improved, and why, but also covers the relevant reporting requirements in the *Evaluation Schedule*;

- presents a balanced and rounded picture of the school;

- gives well-chosen examples or observations that show you know the school;

- allows opportunities for discussion and clarification of the inspection findings;

- avoids giving detailed advice to the school about how to tackle the improvements that are needed.

125   It is expected that all oral reporting will proceed smoothly and professionally and that feedback will be of value to staff and governors alike. If, however, the behaviour of those at a feedback meeting makes it impossible to proceed with a sensible professional dialogue, you as the registered inspector have the right to confine the feedback simply to the main findings of the inspection and the key issues for action. In extreme cases, you have the right not to proceed with the oral report.

126   The use of tape recorders by headteachers, governing bodies and individual teachers at feedback meetings is entirely at the discretion of the registered inspector. It is reasonable for you not to proceed with a feedback meeting if there is any insistence on their use against your will. OFSTED has no objection to the tape recording of feedback meetings if the registered inspector agrees.

THE REPORT AND THE SUMMARY OF THE REPORT

STANDARDS OF REPORTING

127　The inspection report must be a carefully considered, clearly written and well-checked document of high quality. It must relay the inspection findings as unequivocal judgements in clear, straightforward language so that:

- parents, governors, the staff of the school and other readers get a clear picture of the quality and standards of the school, an understanding of its strengths and weaknesses, and insights into why the school achieves as it does;

- the school has a good basis for subsequent action to improve standards and the quality of education.

128　The report should reflect the individual school. It is unique to the school and must, on no account, duplicate in whole or in part the text of earlier reports, however similar the school. The report must follow the structure set out in the *Evaluation Schedule* but its content, wording and style should not be written to any pre-determined formula. Key judgements must be absolutely clear, and consistent with the oral feedback given to the school and governors. Reasons for judgements should be given to enable readers to understand why the inspection team has arrived at its views. While judgements should be based on the criteria set out in the *Evaluation Schedule*, the report should focus on strengths and areas where improvement is needed. It is not necessary to allude to each and every criterion in the schedule, or to quote the criteria parrot-fashion.

129　It is essential that the report provides clear interpretations of any performance data and presents the inspection team's judgements about the educational standards achieved by pupils at the school. Overall judgements should be illustrated by reference to the strengths and weaknesses in the areas of learning or different subjects or courses of the curriculum, with particular emphasis based on the core subjects and English, mathematics, science, ICT and PSHE and, where inspected, religious education.

130　The report must explain any apparent inconsistencies, for example where teaching is generally good but achievement is poor.

131　When reporting on the quality of education provided, inspectors must focus, in particular, on the quality of teaching and learning. Other aspects of provision are important only for their effect on the quality of teaching and learning and the educational standards achieved. Where those other aspects of provision are unexceptional, further justification is usually unnecessary. Where there are particular strengths and weaknesses, though, amplification is needed in order to explain why, for example, mathematics teaching is 'outstanding' or leadership is 'weak'.

132　The **summary report** and the section of the report on WHAT SHOULD THE SCHOOL DO TO IMPROVE FURTHER? are particularly important. The summary is the report for parents and needs particularly careful drafting to communicate effectively with a wide readership. It must draw out the key judgements about the school and leave it without any doubt about the strengths and weaknesses of the school. The contents of the summary, particularly the sections on WHAT THE SCHOOL DOES WELL and WHAT COULD BE IMPROVED, must be consistent with the rest of the report.

133   The report, and its summary, must therefore:

- be clear to all its readers, governors or members of the appropriate authority, parents, professionals and the public at large;

- concentrate on evaluating rather than describing what is seen;

- focus on the educational standards achieved and the factors which impact on standards and quality;

- use everyday language, not educational jargon, and be grammatically correct;

- be specific in its judgements;

- use sub-headings, bullet points and other devices where they help to make the messages clear;

- use telling examples drawn from the evidence base to make generalisations understandable and to illustrate what is meant by 'good' or 'poor';

- use words and phrases that enliven the report and convey the individual character of the school.

134   Readers of the summary report will not necessarily read the full report. The summary report must, therefore, be capable of standing alone as a fair and balanced picture of the school, and the steps needed to improve it.

135   The summary report must include the elements specified in the *Evaluation Schedule*. In addition, the summary report must include the standard text specified in the report template issued to inspectors.

136   The report and summary of the report must be produced within six calendar weeks from the end of the inspection and forwarded without delay to the 'appropriate authority' and HMCI as well as persons specified in sections 16 and 20 of the 1996 Act. The 'appropriate authority' must previously have had five working days to comment on the draft version of the report.

STRUCTURE OF REPORTS

137   The sctructure is shown schematically on page 139. All inspection reports include the summary of the report (Part A), the commentary (Part B) and a data section (Part C). **Reports of FULL INSPECTIONS also include a subject section (Part D). Reports of SHORT and FULL INSPECTIONS differ markedly in the structure of the commentary.**

138   In SHORT INSPECTIONS, the commentary is based on the two sections of the summary entitled WHAT THE SCHOOL DOES WELL and WHAT COULD BE IMPROVED. Each of the strengths and weaknesses listed in these two sections of the summary becomes a sub-heading of the commentary. For example, if the first item in WHAT THE SCHOOL DOES WELL is 'Pupils' speaking and listening skills are excellent', then this finding becomes the first sub-heading for the commentary. The commentary of short reports, therefore, does not follow the headings provided by the *Evaluation Schedule*.

139   In FULL INSPECTIONS, the commentary of the report follows the structure set out in the *Evaluation Schedule*.

PRESENTATION OF THE PRE-PUBLICATION REPORT TO THE SCHOOL

140   The school has five working days in which to consider the final, pre-publication draft of the inspection report to check the factual accuracy of its content. *The registered inspector must ensure that the report shown to the school is his or her intended final report and is of publication quality. By this stage it must have taken account of comments made by an editorial reader hired by the contractor.* Showing this report to the school is not meant to be an opportunity to negotiate judgements. The report should contain no surprises. It should reflect precisely the judgements conveyed during oral feedback to the senior managers and the appropriate authority.

REPORTING REQUIREMENTS

REPORT

SUMMARY   +   COMMENTARY

THIS IS PART A OF THE REPORT

- Information about the school
- How good the school is

followed by a list of the main strengths of the school and any weaknesses under the headings:

- What the school does well
- What could be improved

If the school is judged to be underachieving, or is identified as having serious weaknesses or requiring special measures, this should be stated.

- How the school has improved since its last inspection
- Standards
- Pupils' attitudes and values
- Teaching and learning
- Other aspects of the school
- How well is the school led and managed?
- Parents' and carers' views of the school

SHORT INSPECTION

FULL INSPECTION

The summary report must include:
- all statutory reporting requirements;
- required judgements about each of the ☐ headings for sections 1–9 of the *Evaluation Schedule* and, in FULL INSPECTIONS, a summary of the strengths and weaknesses from section 10 of the *Schedule*.

THIS IS PART B OF THE REPORT

A commentary on each of the issues listed in:

- What the school does well
and
- What could be improved

followed by sections on:

- What should the school do to improve further?
- Other specified features (if any)

THIS IS PART C OF THE REPORT

Data tables

Summary of responses to parents' questionnaire

THIS IS PART B OF THE REPORT

- How high are standards?
    The school's results and pupils' achievements
    Pupils' attitudes, values and personal development
- How well are pupils taught?
- How good are the curricular and other opportunities offered to pupils?
- How well does the school care for its pupils?
- How well does the school work in partnership with parents?
- How well is the school led and managed?
- What should the school do to improve further?
- Other specified features (if any)

THIS IS PART C OF THE REPORT

Data tables

Summary of responses to parents' questionnaire

THIS IS PART D OF THE REPORT

- The standards and quality of teaching in areas of the curriculum and subjects

PART 3

USING THE *HANDBOOK* FOR SCHOOL SELF-EVALUATION

SELF-EVALUATION

The school that knows and understands itself is well on the way to solving any problems it has. The school that is ignorant of its weaknesses or will not, or cannot, face up to them is not well-managed. Self-evaluation provides the key to improvement. The ability to generate a commitment among staff to appraise their own work critically, and that of others, is a key test of how well a school is managed.

Effective change and self-evaluation are characterised by openness and consultation and are a regular part of the good school's working life in which everyone is encouraged to participate. Self-evaluation complements inspection with a constant process of identifying priorities for improvement, monitoring provision and evaluating outcomes.

Both inspection and internal evaluation are concerned with providing an accurate appraisal of the quality and standards of the school and diagnosing what needs to be done to improve them. Inspectors have a duty to report, via the governing body, to parents. Schools are encouraged to do the same with their self-evaluation findings.

It is advantageous to base school self-evaluation on the same criteria as those used in all schools by inspectors. A common language has developed about the work of schools, expressed through the criteria. Teachers and governors know that the criteria reflect things that matter.

The guidance on inspection published for inspectors in the first revision of the OFSTED *Handbooks*[2] is accepted by headteachers as a sound basis for evaluation, defining a useful range of criteria to assess the quality and impact of what schools provide for pupils. *School Evaluation Matters*[3] exemplifies and illustrates the work of many schools for whom monitoring and evaluation are central to improvement. *Making the Most of Inspection*[4] helps schools to see external inspection as one aspect of evaluation, which can be actively used to promote improvement.

Self-evaluation is not about being an inspector. By using this guidance you should be able to undertake an annual analysis of the standards and the effectiveness of your actions.

There are four questions that are at the heart of evaluating everything you do:

- **Are all the pupils in my school learning as much as they are capable of learning?**

- **What can I do to find out?**

- **When I answer this question how do I know I am right?**

- **What do I do about it when I have the answer?**

To ensure that self-evaluation has the maximum impact on standards:

- take an objective look at pupils' achievements and pinpoint areas of underachievement;

- account for outcomes in your school by identifying strengths and weaknesses in teaching, before looking at what else you provide to support learning;

---

[2] The OFSTED Handbooks: *Guidance on the Inspection of Nursery, Primary, Secondary and Special Schools*, HMSO 1995.

[3] OFSTED Publications Centre 1998.

[4] OFSTED Publications Centre 1998.

■ use this information to devise the School Improvement (Development) Plan, which is at its best when seen simply as a means to raise standards.

WHAT POINT HAVE YOU REACHED?

In 1997–98 one in five of all schools was judged to be good, or very good, at monitoring and evaluating the quality of its work, and a further one in ten was judged to be satisfactory. Although these proportions show an improvement since the beginning of the OFSTED inspection cycle, there is still substantial work to be done.[5]

Special schools and pupil referral units vary considerably in their management of evaluation. For example, one special school:

effectively uses a range of strategies for monitoring the quality of teaching and of the curriculum. These involve checks on pupils' work, teachers' planning and visits to classrooms to observe practice. The members of the governors' curriculum committee make a valuable contribution by commenting on reports and policy documents, and by making firsthand checks on their progress and implementation.

In another special school, self-evaluation is not on the school's list of urgent tasks because:

the headteacher claims that with his teaching load and other responsibilities there is no time for monitoring, neither is there an expectation that subject co-ordinators or governors will be involved in any self-evaluation activity.

School self-evaluation is about diagnosis and change in the way people work, and this is particularly so for teaching and its impact. But it must carry a 'health warning'. It can be a mistake to 'do a self-evaluation' of the whole school, treating it as one event like 'having an inspection'. It is far better that inspection complements a process of identifying and nibbling away at priorities through regular monitoring and evaluation.

■ **If you have not introduced a strategy for monitoring and evaluating** the work of your school, your area of responsibility, or your own work in the classroom, you will find the *Handbook* particularly helpful.

■ **If some monitoring and evaluation is in place,** this guidance will enable you to assess how effectively you undertake it.

■ **If you feel there is already 'continuous evaluation',** you will be able to check whether such blanket coverage is concealing some prime suspects for investigation.

■ **If you feel there is little we can tell you about self-evaluation,** then we should be pleased if you would tell us more about what you do.

Wherever you are up to, *Form S4* (on the CD-ROM attached to this *Handbook*) is about self-evaluation. It is for the inspection team, but we believe that many headteachers and governors or the appropriate authority will find *Form S4* a useful basis for the regular evaluation of the progress their school is making, across all its work, whether or not it is being inspected.

---

[5] Data taken from *Primary Education 1994–98*, HMSO 1999; and *Secondary Education 1993–97*, HMSO 1998.

WHERE DO YOU BEGIN?

There are several possible starting points. They may include:

■ **areas identified by senior management or the governing body as needing improvement;**

> which may have arisen as a result of monitoring performance, evidence of problems, a survey of parents or staff, or for other reasons;

■ **interest by one or more particular staff;**

> in which case they should be helped and encouraged, and their work used as a pilot for wider adoption;

■ **a known area of strength or weakness in the school;**

> which can then be evaluated and the reasons for success, or lack of it, diagnosed;

■ **an inspection report;**

> in which issues are identified that need to be investigated further as a basis for action.

Two of the most systematic spurs to self-evaluation are the appraisal of teachers, and the monitoring and analysis of achievement. Inspectors start from the latter point, as illustrated in Part 2 of this *Handbook*. Monitoring and analysing achievement have the advantage of illuminating where to focus your evaluative effort. Appraisal, on the other hand, applies to all and is a major undertaking.

EVALUATING STANDARDS

Start with monitoring standards and related matters. Strong internal reviews look first at key measurable outcomes. Your monitoring of measurable outcomes, such as standards, should result in evaluation that examines the quality and impact of what you provide. For instance, use:

■ pupils' attainment on entry;

■ analysis of test and examination results of external accreditation of pupils' work;

■ a study of ethnicity and gender balances in your results;

■ test analysis, where appropriate;

■ monitoring to know how many pupils reach their targets;

■ standards in the school measured against other schools, where this is appropriate;

■ value-added information;

■ an analysis of pupils' progress made by different groups of pupils across Key Stages;

■ an analysis of attendance and punctuality patterns;

■ interviews with staff about their classes and the pupils they teach or support, and other work they undertake;

■ a review of governors' or the appropriate authority's attitude to standards in your school;

■ questions to parents about what they think of what your school does.

You will want to: analyse pupils' attainment and learning need on entry; predict the maximum possible gains in knowledge, understanding and skills for pupils; and set appropriate targets; determine how these can best be achieved; analyse performance at the end of each year and Key Stage; record the progress made by pupils, and decide where, if anywhere, improvements are needed.

EVALUATING TEACHING

The monitoring, evaluation and support of teaching are central to school effectiveness and improvement. Systematic monitoring of teaching by both teachers and learning support assistants through classroom observation is relatively rare. As a result, in many schools senior staff lack the knowledge they need if they are to help raise standards. The observation and evaluation of teaching and learning should be based on clear and understood criteria. Section 3 of Part 1 of this *Handbook* – HOW WELL ARE PUPILS TAUGHT? – gives national criteria for judging teaching and learning, together with guidance on their application.

The section entitled *Making Judgements* states clearly the characteristics of very good teaching and unsatisfactory teaching. You may initially want to focus on one subject or aspect of teaching.

You will see that the overriding consideration for evaluating the quality of teaching is how well pupils learn. This is judged not only by assessing their knowledge, understanding and skills, but by looking at the extent of their engagement in the lesson, the pace of their work and the demands made on them. If these are good, decide what the features of teaching are which have this effect. If the converse is true, you need to diagnose what is not working well enough and consider what could be done to improve matters. Evaluation and setting an agenda for development are starting points, but are of limited value unless the monitoring of classroom teaching is systematic; carried out to agreed criteria; and the outcomes discussed with teachers.

The section on *Guidance on using the Evaluation Schedule*, helps you to know what to look for in your lesson observations. You can use the *Evaluation Forms* on the CD-ROM to record the information. Before the observation ensure that teachers know what your focus will be. Try to make sure that it arises from the monitoring you have done of standards. During lesson observations, record what teachers do well and less well, always judge their work by the impact it has on pupils' learning. Note how pupils respond during the lesson, watch how their attitudes to learning and their behaviour influence the standards they reach. Try to record how much learning has taken place during your observation, measured by talking with pupils, examining their work and looking back through their work to see where they have come from, and gauge their progress.

As you conclude an observation decide how effective the lesson was overall, which parts worked best and which – if any – did not work so well. Did all pupils in the class gain from the demands made of them? Did all the teaching techniques and elements of the lesson contribute well to the intended outcomes? Where were the strengths and weaknesses? What could be done more effectively in future?

FEEDING BACK AFTER OBSERVING LESSONS, AND ONGOING SUPPORT

It is essential to have an agreed format for feeding back your considered evaluation of teaching. Schools may use different ways of doing this. Some do it collectively, with the group of staff involved, others individually. The guidance provided for inspectors in Part 2 of this *Handbook*, on giving feedback, may be helpful to you.

Evaluation should lead to personal or team agendas becoming more effective. These should include targets for improvement, against which progress may be monitored through regular structured follow-up observations to see if the targets have been realised. It is important that management supports these agendas in all possible ways, which may include professional development, the acquisition of resources and the opportunity to visit teachers in other classes or schools.

PERFORMANCE MANAGEMENT AND LEADING IMPROVEMENT

If you are a headteacher or governor in a maintained school or PRU, performance management is now an integral part of your work. The 1999 *School Teachers' Pay and Conditions Document* [6] stipulates that headteachers' professional duties include:

> *evaluating the standards of teaching and learning in the school, and ensuring that proper standards of professional performance are established and maintained.*

Many would argue that all staff with management responsibilities have similar obligations. Performance is rightly associated with the standards achieved and the quality of learning. Performance management policies will centre on the assessment of teaching, and analysis of pupils' progress and learning, to guide the setting of targets for improvement and development over the next year. The governing body has responsibility for appraising the performance of the headteacher, setting appropriate targets for the headteacher and deciding on performance-related pay for the headteacher and staff.

Performance management is most effective where there is:

- strong, well-motivated and clear-sighted leadership;

- rigorous analysis of standards;

- continuous monitoring and evaluation of teaching and learning;

- wholehearted commitment from staff to the school and to self-improvement;

- a set of easily understood objectives and reasonable but challenging targets at all levels;

- plenty of support for development and improvement;

- good management of resources, including financial incentives and rewards that maximise performance.

The impact of your management and leadership and of those who support you in running the school will dictate how governors, staff, pupils and parents see the quality of your performance as the headteacher. The *Evaluation Schedule* section 7, HOW WELL IS THE SCHOOL LED AND MANAGED?, will help you to review and improve your own performance and that of any senior colleagues you may have. Remember that you may not be the best person to lead such an evaluation. Involve teachers new to the school, parents, governors and staff. Some schools also involve pupils in school evaluation. The section headed *Making Judgements* makes clear the vital features of good leaders and managers, and the section on leadership and management will help you to find ways of measuring the impact of what you and your colleagues do, and how it benefits pupils.

---

[6] *School Teachers' Pay and Conditions Document 1999*, paragraph 43.7.

As the headteacher, you are strongly influential in providing a culture in which the cycle of self-evaluation and development is valued, understood, published and communicated. It is crucially important that you assure its effectiveness and ensure that everyone in the school is involved in, and committed to, their own learning as part of maximising pupils' achievements. Thus to be at your best you, your staff and governors should be reflective and analytical when weighing up the value, or effectiveness, of what you provide.

USING INSPECTION TO COMPLEMENT SELF-EVALUATION

Inspection, well used, complements good self-evaluation. During an inspection there will be a number of opportunities for you and your staff to: test your perceptions of the school against those of impartial, external evaluators; receive feedback; and discuss the quality and standards being achieved. Making the most of these opportunities, and the discussions and professional debates during the more formal feedback meetings, will provide additional valuable information to add to your own evaluation of your school. Together with the key issues, all these points will help you and your governors to prepare an action plan and direct your school improvement planning.

As with the outcomes of your self-evaluation activities, use inspection to celebrate success. It is essential to recognise where the school is doing well, and to compliment those involved, as well as to tackle matters that need to be improved. It is particularly important to be positive and forward-looking after the inspection is over and the report has arrived, or after any phase of intensive evaluation, in order to combat the sense of anticlimax which can prevail, even with the most resounding endorsement of the school.

SCHOOL SELF-EVALUATION IN A NUTSHELL

Start now

Accept that we can all improve

Place the raising of standards at the heart of all your planning

Measure standards

Compare yourself with others

Regularly observe each other teaching to a set of agreed and rigorous criteria

Evaluate the effect that teaching has on learning

Be completely open in feeding back what you find

Think, discuss and consult

Set targets for everyone's improvement

Ensure that action is supported, monitored and reviewed

Never stop evaluating

Example 1

Specific focus on the skills of communication (speaking and listening) in a special school

The headteacher and all staff of a special school for pupils with severe, profound and multiple learning difficulties had recently received in-service work on improving communication skills, including signing. The senior management team wanted to monitor its impact and were particularly concerned to find out if the staff communicated consistently with individual pupils. By agreement, they decided to monitor how effectively staff interacted with pupils at Key Stages 3 and 4.

The first question the school sought to answer was:

Do we use consistent approaches when communicating with pupils in all lessons?

The school used:

- *the OFSTED criteria for judging the quality of teaching;*

- *prompts from the recently modified scheme of work for English;*

- *parts of pupils' individual education plans;*

- Evidence Forms *to record lesson observations.*

Evidence came from:

- *teachers' plans;*

- *observations of each class (4) taught by at least three different members of staff;*

- *observations at lunchtime and break times.*

How and when the evidence was gathered:

- *the English co-ordinator compiled a list of each pupils' individual targets in relation to listening and speaking (or signing) and noted what were the agreed approaches to be used and the expected response for each pupil;*

- *over a period of two weeks the head and deputy each observed the classes twice for whole lessons, making sure all staff who taught the pupils were observed;*

- *the head and deputy each observed lunchtime supervisors both during and after lunch;*

- *evidence from a staff meeting was gathered about the different ways staff make sure that each pupil is spoken to and how responses are recorded.*

The evidence was analysed:

- *by the headteacher and co-ordinator, using* Evidence Forms *to examine how consistently staff communicated with pupils in accordance with agreed targets;*

- *by noting any similarities or differences in the approaches used by staff by looking at the* Evidence Forms *completed for each class when taught by different teachers;*

- *by noting the most effective and least effective aspects of teaching in ensuring that pupils were required to listen and make responses. They matched this to the evidence gathered from the staff meeting on the individual approaches used by staff.*

(continued overleaf)

(Example continued)

The evidence showed that:

- *signing was used consistently by all staff apart from in food technology, where the teacher was too preoccupied with the task in hand, at the expense of ensuring that all pupils were spoken to;*

- *pupils who communicate orally without signing were not consistently asked to speak at the level set in their targets;*

- *most lunchtime supervisors were very effective in maintaining consistency of approaches when pupils were eating and when out in the playground at lunchtime;*

- *the teachers who were the most consistent had previously set out simple but clear plans for the lesson and briefed special support assistants clearly;*

- *teachers who were less consistent were unclear about the main purpose of their lessons and had a few prompts to question each pupil about what they had learned.*

Staff were shown the Evidence Forms *and agreed with the findings.*

Improvements proposed to staff:

- *proposals were made to each individual member of staff arising from the evidence of each lesson on how to maintain or improve their approaches;*

- *the co-ordinator agreed to make available ideas and plans used by the most effective teachers for all to see.*

Monitoring implications:

- *targets were agreed with individual teachers for measuring improvements;*

- *further lessons over time were to be observed to ensure that improvements were put in place;*

- *the English co-ordinator would visit each colleague to check that agreed targets were being implemented;*

- *regular staff meetings would be held to remind staff about individual pupils' needs and targets.*

PART 4

ANNEXES

ANNEX 1

JUDGING BEST VALUE PRINCIPLES AND FINANCIAL MANAGEMENT IN SCHOOLS

There is a statutory duty on local authorities (in general, not just LEAs) to obtain best value by securing economic, efficient and effective services. The best value framework, within which local authorities are required to respond to local needs and make decisions locally, primarily focuses on the balance between cost and quality in striving continuously to improve services.

The best value approach does not apply statutorily to governing bodies in their use of delegated and devolved budgets. However, governing bodies are required to set targets to raise standards, are expected to provide a good-quality public service, and spend public money wisely. Schools are accountable for balancing *costs* (in terms of economy and efficiency) and *effectiveness* (in terms of their performance and the quality of what they provide) as required by the best value framework. To achieve this schools need to demonstrate that they apply best value principles in arriving at decisions about all their activities, especially how the financial resources delegated to them are managed.

Your task on inspection is, in light of all the available evidence, to evaluate and report on how effectively the school applies best value principles in its management and use of resources.

INSPECTION AND THE BEST VALUE FRAMEWORK

Inspecting the use of the best value framework fits easily within the overall inspection process. Both require attention to be given to evaluating the school's performance and its management and planning processes. One sign of effective planning is, for example, a challenging and appropriately costed school development plan.

The best value framework covers four principles (summarised as the four 'Cs'), each of which is linked to specific requirements in the *Evaluation Schedule*:

■ Compare;

■ Challenge;

■ Consult;

■ Compete.

The following are examples of questions you may wish to use, grouped under the headings related to the four principles.

COMPARE: Comparison of performance against that of all schools and similar schools is difficult for special schools and PRUs. Many schools and units have strategies, such as networking, to combat such isolation. They also have access to specialist advice and inspection to judge how well they are doing. Find out the extent to which the school asks itself, and answers, such questions as:

- *What is the quality of education provided by similar schools?*

- *How do our standards compare with theirs?*

- *Are we a relatively high performer?*

- *Do we cost more or less than others?*

- *Why?*

In independent schools, you should only consider whether public money, in the form of fees, is used appropriately to provide the services purchased. Guidance on evaluating value for money appears in Part 1 of this *Handbook*.

CHALLENGE: This is about whether the school challenges itself about the services it provides. Does the school take steps, for example, to find out whether what it provides is what is needed? Could some aspects be more effectively provided, for example in a mainstream school, perhaps with outreach support? How great is the commitment to the re-entry of pupils into local schools, particularly pupils in PRUs? Find out the extent to which the school asks itself such questions as:

- *Why are we doing this?*

- *Is it what people want?*

- *What is the evidence about level of need?*

- *Could someone else do it differently, or better?*

CONSULT: This is about being clear what the school community wants. When considering major changes or spending decisions, involving the curriculum provided or other major developments, does the school seek the views of those most concerned and how does it respond to those views? This means asking or getting feedback from staff, parents, pupils and others on:

- *what they want the school to do;*

- *what they think of proposed changes or major expenditure;*

- *whether they are happy with, or at, the school;*

- *what is in their best interests.*

Did the school consult parents, for example, when drawing up a post-inspection action plan? or when changing the balance of the curriculum? Or does it just announce such matters? Increasingly, schools use questionnaires to survey parents; many also periodically seek the views of pupils.

COMPETE: Competition is concerned both with whether the school is doing anything which could be better provided by someone else, and with the strategic use of resources and getting best value for expenditure. Does the school have proper financial administration procedures, including competitive tendering for significant expenditure? Examples might include supply and part-time staff, in-service training, expenditure on equipment and maintenance contracts. Is purchasing on a fair and open basis or through personal connection, or is one supplier used regardless of price? The school should be asking questions like:

- *Are we providing the service at the right price?*

- *Could we or others provide it at a better price?*

- *What do the users of this service want?*

- *What is in the best interest of pupils and parents?*

- *How does the school ensure it receives the most economic, efficient and effective service from those who provide services to pupils and staff?*

You will need to determine whether the school manages its decision-making and assesses the impact on standards of its spending and other decisions in ways that reflect the best value framework. You will need to find out how it balances *costs* (in terms of economy and efficiency) and *effectiveness* (in terms of the performance of the school and the quality of what it provides). This has implications for how you gather and test the evidence from the whole of the inspection, for example your analysis of performance in section 2 and your evaluation of school provision in sections 3 and 4 of the *Evaluation Schedule*.

It is not, however, for inspectors to judge whether best value is being positively achieved; such a judgement is a matter for local accountability. What is required of inspectors is to make information available to parents and other local people about whether the school is applying the best value principle effectively and for them to come to a view about whether best value is being achieved.

Some schools will be more familiar with the principles of best value than others, although some of the elements, such as consultation and comparison, are commonplace in well-managed schools. Schools have been familiar with the value-for-money judgements made by inspectors for years. Best value reflects an attitude to management. You should explore the principles with the school as part of your evaluation of standards, the curriculum, and partnership with parents and management. Best value can be seen as a theme that runs across the different strands of inspection or school evaluation.

Bear in mind that working to these principles is an *expectation* of schools, not a *requirement* – as it is with local authorities. All inspection reports should indicate, however, the extent to which the work of the school reflects best value principles, summarising areas of strength and weakness. Whatever references are made in other areas of the report, your evaluation should be summarised in the leadership and management section.

If, on the evidence of the inspection, the performance of the school is not high enough, you are required to highlight your concerns in the report. These may include the extent to which the school does or does not apply best value principles effectively. These concerns must be set out in the section WHAT SHOULD THE SCHOOL DO TO IMPROVE FURTHER? and in the summary of the report. These concerns will be reflected in the inspection team's judgement about the school's capacity for improvement and its overall effectiveness, especially the summative judgement about whether the school is underachieving; has serious weaknesses in one or more areas; or is failing, or likely to fail, to give its pupils an acceptable standard of education and requires special measures.

BEST VALUE AND AUDIT

A feature of good school management is the use made of performance review to evaluate how well it is doing and to identify what action is needed to secure improvement. A key task of inspection is to evaluate the school's financial planning, and how it links its strategic use of resources, including specific grants and additional funding, with educational priorities. Many of these areas are covered in financial audit and you will need to make full use of the audit reports in coming to judgements about *costs* and *effectiveness* within the best value framework.

Audit and inspection are complementary processes. The following table identifies key common areas, based on the guidance on schemes of delegation under Fair Funding arrangements.[7] You will need to consider them in the light of evidence from inspection (including budget statements), taking full account of the school's most recent audit. The suggested format will help you organise the evidence and focus your judgements.

---

[7] See guidance issued by the Secretary of State under schedule 14 of the School Standards and Framework Act 1998.

Questions for audit	Areas for audit/inspection[8]	Questions for inspection
The focus of auditors will be on whether the governing body and the school:		*Inspectors will need to evaluate whether the governing body and school:*
• have set out clear delegation arrangements	**Delegation of powers to the headteacher**	• use delegation wisely
• maintain up-to-date inventories	**Control of assets**	• keep track of its resources
• have a register which is regularly updated and available for scrutiny	**Register of business interests**	• have a register available and whether its contents reveal any significant issues that require following up by others
• have a scheme to cover these arrangements which is used effectively within the best value framework	**Purchasing, tendering and contracting requirements**	• use these arrangements effectively and within the best value framework
• use buy-back services which fall within the scheme of delegation	**Buy-back of services from the LEA or elsewhere**	• effectively use support and other services purchased from the LEA or elsewhere
• regularly and properly have audits carried out	**Audits**	• have acted upon the recommendations to good effect
• submit the budget plan on time and accurately	**Budget plans**	• reflect in the budget plan the priorities set out in the school development plan; if not, why not?
• engage in any irregular spending and/or spending outside the scheme of delegation	**Spending for the purposes of the school**	• spend to reflect the school's purposes and identified priorities for improvement
• have arrangements for ensuring earmarked funds are used for their designated purposes	**Central funds and earmarking funds for designated purposes**	• monitor and evaluate their spending decisions within a best value framework • use earmarked funds only for their designated purposes
• undertake capital spending within regulations	**Capital spending**	• use capital spending appropriately and in line with priorities in the school development plan • monitor and evaluate capital spending decisions within a best value framework

[8] See guidance issued by the Secretary of State under schedule 14 of the School Standards and Framework Act 1998.

Questions for audit	Areas for audit/inspection	Questions for inspection
The focus of auditors will be on whether the governing body and the school:		*Inspectors will need to evaluate whether the governing body and school:*
• use their borrowing powers within the scheme of delegation	**Borrowing by schools**	• use borrowing wisely and in line with priorities set out in the school development plan
• ensure any income accrues to the budget • ensure that any cross-subsidy, for example from community or other use of facilities, has no net cost to the school's budget	**Income**	• ensure that arrangements for letting the building for community use benefit the school educationally and are in line with priorities set out in the school development plan
• have a plan for the use of budget surpluses	**Budget surpluses**	• plan to use budget surpluses wisely and in line with priorities set out in the school development plan
• have a justifiable deficit budget, that is licensed by the LEA and linked to an agreed plan for retrieving the budget deficit	**Budget deficits**	• have a deficit budget due to inefficient spending or for other reasons • have a plan for retrieving the deficit which is educationally justifiable and in line with priorities set out in the school development plan
• have a statement setting out what steps are to be taken to ensure best value, and whether the school's management and use of resources adhere to the declared intentions	**Best value**	• apply best value principles effectively in their management and use of resources

Evaluation of best value and financial management should be informed by the items in the right-hand column, although it may not be possible to investigate all of them rigorously.

USE OF PERFORMANCE INDICATORS

You will need to make full use of a range of performance indicators to ju[dge] the best value framework consistently and effectively in its financial plan[ning and] resources. These indicators will be helpful if set alongside the school's ow[n] (including any value-added analysis undertaken) and the school's accoun[t] taken by governors, the headteacher and staff about the use of resources.

ANNEX 2

SCHOOLS REQUIRING SPECIAL MEASURES, SCHOOLS WITH SERIOUS WEAKNESSES, AND UNDERACHIEVING SCHOOLS

On every inspection, as a team, you must consider whether the school is failing, or likely to fail, to give its pupils an acceptable standard of education, and therefore requires special measures.

If you judge that the school is providing an acceptable standard of education, the next step is to consider whether it nevertheless has serious weaknesses.

You also need to consider whether the school, though not identified as having serious weaknesses, is judged to be underachieving.

These judgements must be reported using the prescribed wording, and specific procedures must be followed.

BACKGROUND

The School Inspections Act 1996 (the 1996 Act) states that: 'Special measures are required to be taken in relation to a school if the school is failing or likely to fail to give its pupils an acceptable standard of education' (section 13(9)).

Towards the end of an inspection, as a team, you must consider whether the school is failing, or likely to fail, to give its pupils an acceptable standard of education (Framework, paragraph 33). If you reach this view, and HMCI agrees, then special measures will be required.

If you reach the view that the school is providing its pupils with an acceptable standard of education, you should then and only then consider whether it nevertheless has serious weaknesses.

JUDGING THAT A SCHOOL REQUIRES SPECIAL MEASURES

The possibility that a school may be failing or likely to fail to give its pupils an acceptable standard of education should be considered initially during the pre-inspection analysis of data, indicators and other evidence about the school's performance.

It is uncomfortable coming to a judgement that a school is failing or likely to fail, but it is one which you must not shirk. You must not take the easier course represented by the judgement that the school has serious weaknesses if the evidence points to the conclusion that the school is not providing an acceptable standard of education.

Factors to consider

One feature alone is unlikely to result in a judgement that a school requires special measures, but where you find low standards and poor learning, risk to pupils or the likelihood of a breakdown of discipline, the school will normally require special measures.

The following questions are a guide to the judgement that a school requires special measures.

a.	**Education standards achieved:**	
i.	Is there low achievement in the subjects of the curriculum by the majority of pupils or consistently among particular groups of pupils?	Yes/No
ii.	Is there poor learning and progress in the subjects of the curriculum by the majority of pupils or consistently among particular groups of pupils?	Yes/No
iii.	Is there insufficient external accreditation of achievement?	Yes/No
iv.	Are the National Curriculum assessment and other accredited results poor?	Yes/No
v.	Does the school handle disruptive behaviour ineffectively?	Yes/No
vi.	Is there no discernable improvement or even repression in pupils' behaviour compared with the behaviour on entry to the school?	Yes/No
vii.	Are there high levels of exclusions?	Yes/No
viii.	Are there significant levels of racial tension or harassment?	Yes/No
ix.	Is there poor attendance and failure to improve by a substantial proportion of pupils?	Yes/No
x.	Is there poor attendance and failure to improve by particular groups of pupils?	Yes/No
xi.	Is there a high level of truancy or of pupils absconding?	Yes/No

b.	**Quality of education provided:**	
i.	Is there a high proportion of unsatisfactory teaching?	Yes/No
ii.	Are there low expectations of pupils?	Yes/No
iii.	Is there failure to implement the National Curriculum or a suitable curriculum?	Yes/No
iv.	Is there poor provision for pupils' spiritual, moral, social and cultural development?	Yes/No
v.	Are pupils at physical or emotional risk from other pupils or adults in the school?	Yes/No
vi.	Are there abrasive and confrontational relationships between staff and pupils?	Yes/No

c.	**The leadership and management of the school:**	
i.	Is the headteacher and/or the senior management team and/or the governors or key members of the appropriate authority ineffective?	Yes/No
ii.	Is there significant loss of confidence in the headteacher by the parents and/or the governors or appropriate authority	
iii.	Is there demoralisation and disenchantment amongst staff	
iv.	Are there high levels of staff turnover or absence?	
v.	Is there poor management?	
vi.	Is inefficient use made of the resources available to the sch	
vii.	Does the school apply principles of best value in its use of	

You may also find the following forms useful in arriving at decisions:

EDUCATIONAL STANDARDS ACHIEVED	serious concern	some concern	no concern
Achievement in:			
English/communication– including literacy			
Mathematics – including numeracy			
Science			
Design and technology			
Information technology			
History			
Geography			
Modern foreign languages			
Music			
Art			
PE			
In NC subjects or curriculum overall			
Religious education – special schools only			
PSHE			
Post-16 provision			
Other curricular provision			
National test/examination results			
Behaviour			
Level of exclusions			
Level of racial tension or harassment			
Attendance			
Truancy			

QUALITY OF EDUCATION PROVIDED	serious concern	some concern	no concern
Teaching			
Expectations of pupils			
Implementation of the curriculum			
Provision for pupils' SMSC development			
Pupils at physical/emotional risk from other pupils			
Pupils at physical/emotional risk from adults			
Relationships between staff and pupils			
LEADERSHIP AND MANAGEMENT OF THE SCHOOL			
Effectiveness of headteacher/teacher in charge			
Effectiveness of other senior managers			
Effectiveness of the governors/appropriate authority			
Confidence in the headteacher by staff			
Confidence in the headteacher by parents			
Confidence in the headteacher by governors			
Demoralisation and disenchantment among staff			
Level of staff turnover/absence			
Management/use made of available resources			
Principles of best value applied by the school			
School improvement since last inspection			
Ability to secure necessary improvements			

A school will be likely to fail if it:

- is close to the point where it would be judged to be failing;

- is declining rapidly in one or a number of important areas;

- is in decline and this is not being checked by the senior managers and appropriate authority;

- is in a precarious state where the management is ineffective and therefore the quality of education is likely to decline;

- has many weaknesses and had made insufficient progress since the last inspection.

Procedures to be followed

If the accumulating evidence suggests that the school may require special measures, you can get further guidance during office hours from the School Improvement Division in OFSTED (telephone 020 7421 6594). If, as a team, you reach the judgement that the school is failing or likely to fail, and therefore requires special measures, the registered inspector must:

■ inform the School Improvement Division in OFSTED before the school is told of the judgement;

■ before leaving the school at the end of the inspection, tell the headteacher orally either that in the view of the inspection team there are serious deficiencies and that the team is considering whether the school is failing, or likely to fail, to give its pupils an acceptable standard of education, or that the inspection team has reached a corporate judgement that the school is failing or likely to fail to give its pupils an acceptable standard of education;

■ when giving oral reports to the senior management team and the appropriate authority, state that the corporate judgement of the inspection team is that the school is failing, or likely to fail, to give its pupils an acceptable standard of education. The following form of words could be used:

> *I am of the opinion that special measures are required in relation to this school because it is failing (or likely to fail) to give its pupils an acceptable standard of education. In accordance with section 13(2) of the School Inspections Act 1996 I shall send a draft report to HMCI and will await his judgement on whether he agrees or not that the school requires special measures.*

■ explain that submission of the draft report to OFSTED may delay the issue of the report to the appropriate authority. The maximum delay is three months from the date when the report was due;

■ use *Form 1* at the end of this section to inform the School Improvement Division in OFSTED of the team's decision;

■ submit to OFSTED, but not to the school, the draft report and any other papers that are required as quickly as possible and by the agreed date, and always within five weeks of the end of the inspection.

What happens next?

HMI will consider the evidence and may visit the school before recommending to HMCI whether or not to agree that the school requires special measures. Whenever possible, if a visit is to take place, it will be within three working weeks of the inspection. The purpose of the visit will be to confirm or otherwise that special measures are required; HMI will not be re-inspecting the school.

If you are the registered inspector, you must ensure that all the evidence collected during the inspection is available for scrutiny by HMCI. It is probable that, on behalf of HMCI, the School Improvement Division will ask you to provide:

■ the school prospectus;

■ a plan of the school and a map showing its location;

■ timetables and a copy of any key that is necessary to be able to interpret the timetables;

■ the draft report and summary;

■ the completed *Record of Corporate Judgements* (including JRF grades), all completed *Inspection Notebooks* (including subject JRF grades), and *Evidence Forms;*

■ *Forms S1–S4;*

■ a note of the main issues raised at the parents' meeting and in the parents' questionnaire responses.

When HMI have scrutinised the evidence and, in some cases, visited the school, they report to HMCI. He will decide whether or not he agrees with the team's opinion and will tell you of his decision.

If HMCI agrees with the judgement that the school is failing or likely to fail, the following form of words should be used in the summary report:

> *In accordance with section 13(7) of the School Inspections Act 1996 I am of the opinion, and HMCI agrees, that special measures are required in relation to this school.*

If HMCI does not agree, the reasons will be explained and you will be given the opportunity to discuss HMCI's decision. Three options are open to you:

■ accept HMCI's decision and amend the report by removing the opinion that the school requires special measures, and then issue the report;

■ decide to issue the report without amendment. Special measures will not apply and you must then use the following form of words in the main findings of the report and in the summary:

> *In accordance with section 13(7) of the School Inspection Act 1996, I am of the opinion, but HMCI disagrees, that special measures are required in relation to this school.*

■ prepare further drafts for HMCI to consider, incorporating the opinion that the school is failing, or likely to fail. If HMCI still disagrees after considering subsequent drafts, you may decide to issue the report and summary without further amendment, but must state that HMCI disagrees with you using the form of words above. The report and summary must be substantially the same as the latest drafts sent to HMCI. Special measures will not apply.

JUDGING THAT A SCHOOL HAS A SERIOUS WEAKNESSES

Factors to consider

If, as a team, you reach the view that the school is giving an acceptable standard of education, you should then consider whether or not it nevertheless has serious weaknesses in one or more areas of its work. In doing so, you should refer to the same characteristics as those you considered when deciding whether or not the school is giving an acceptable standard of education. You should make your judgements in the light of the findings as a whole, but should normally view the following weaknesses as significant:

- low standards of achievement, particularly in the core subjects;
- unsatisfactory teaching in about one in eight lessons;
- ineffective leadership and/or management.

Procedures to be followed

The registered inspector should tell the headteacher at the end of the inspection either that the team's view is that there are deficiencies and that it is considering whether the school has serious weaknesses, or that it has reached the judgement that the school has serious weaknesses. You must tell the School Improvement Division in OFSTED of your decision by telephone (020 7421 6594) before you tell the school, and subsequently send OFSTED the attached *Form 2*.

You should use a very clear form of words in the summary report. The words 'This school has serious weaknesses' must be included.

A copy of the final report should be sent to the School Improvement Division at the same time as it is sent to the school.

For further information and guidance about special measures or serious weaknesses, contact:

School Improvement Division
OFSTED
Alexandra House
33 Kingsway
London WC2B 6SE

Telephone: 020 7421 6594

JUDGING THAT A SCHOOL IS UNDERACHIEVING

A judgement about whether a school is underachieving will be made, in appropriate circumstances, as part of both SHORT and FULL INSPECTIONS.

Factors to consider

The judgement should be made by considering:

- the effectiveness of the school;
- improvement since the last inspection;
- the performance of the school in comparison with schools in similar contexts.

It should be made on the basis of an analysis **pupils' achievements** in relation to their records and **inspection judgements** about how well they are learning, and in relation to key features of their personal development.

Inspection judgements

The inspection team's judgements about the quality of pupils' learning, their behaviour and personal development; teaching; leadership and management; and care of pupils will explain why pupils are making insufficient progress. Significant pointers might be:

Teaching and learning

- where the percentage of good or better teaching is low;
- where the capacity of the teaching to challenge and inspire pupils is judged unsatisfactory, for particular groups of pupils such as pupils with profound and multiple learning difficulties (PMLD), even if the teaching overall is satisfactory;
- where the methods used to enable all pupils to learn effectively are judged unsatisfactory, although the teaching is judged satisfactory overall;
- where the extent to which pupils show interest in their work, to concentrate and think and learn for themselves is judged unsatisfactory, although pupils' learning of key skills is judged satisfactory overall.

Leadership and management

- where the monitoring, evaluation and development of teaching is judged unsatisfactory;
- where the shared commitment to improvement and the capacity to succeed are judged unsatisfactory;
- where the school's targets are not appropriate and/or progress towards meeting them is unsatisfactory.

School improvement

■ where the judgement that the school has improved since the last inspection is barely satisfactory, overall, with specific and identifiable reservations based on the previous report and other sources of evidence.

The **overall judgement** *that a school is underachieving would be based on:*

■ pupils' achievement not being as good as it could be;

■ evidence that pupils' progress is less than might be reasonably expected, but not to the extent of being a serious weakness;

■ significant concerns about aspects of **teaching, learning, leadership and management**, although these concerns are not acute enough to merit a judgement of serious weaknesses overall.

Procedures to be followed

The registered inspector should tell the headteacher at the end of the inspection either that the team's view is that it is considering whether the school is underachieving, or that it has reached the judgement that the school is underachieving. You must tell the School Improvement Division in OFSTED of your decision by telephone (020 7421 6594) before you tell the school, and subsequently send OFSTED the attached *Form 2*. You should use the words 'This school is underachieving' in the summary report. A copy of the final report should be sent to the School Improvement Division at the same time as it is sent to the school.

For further information and guidance about underachieving schools, contact:

School Improvement Division
OFSTED
Alexandra House
33 Kingsway
London WC2B 6SE

Telephone: 020 7421 6594

RECOMMENDATION FOR SPECIAL MEASURES

This form must be used by **all** lead inspectors to confirm the judgement that the school requires special measures. **Immediately the school has been informed of the decision, this form must be sent to:**

Head of the School Improvement Division
OFSTED
Alexandra House
Room 802
33 Kingsway
London WC2B 6SE

Inspection Number ....

Date of inspection ..../.........../...........

School name ....

Village/town ....

Status ....

Local Education Authority ....

Name of lead inspector ....
[RgI] [AI] [HMI] (delete as appropriate)

Date when report and summary are due ..../.........../...........

I am of the opinion that special measures are required in relation to this school, since it is failing/likely to fail to give its pupils an acceptable standard of education. The reasons for this opinion are:

1

2

3

4

(Please continue on separate sheet if necessary.)

I will send you drafts of the report and the summary by ..../.........../...........

I confirm that I will report in these terms to the senior management team of the school and to the governors.

Signed ....

Name (please print) .... Date ..../.........../.........

Telephone number ....

Address ....

CONFIRMATION OF SERIOUS WEAKNESSES *OR* THAT THE SCHOOL IS UNDERACHIEVING

This form must be used by **all** lead inspectors to confirm the judgement that the school has serious weaknesses **or** is underachieving. **Immediately the school has been informed of the decision, this form must be sent to:**

Head of the School Improvement Division
OFSTED
Alexandra House
Room 802
33 Kingsway
London WC2B 6SE

Date of inspection ..../.........../...........

Date when report and summary are due ..../.........../...........

I will send you the final report and the summary by ..../.........../...........

School name ....

Village/town ....

Status ....

Local Education Authority ....

Name of lead inspector ....
[RgI] [AI] [HMI] (delete as appropriate)

Delete as appropriate:

I am of the opinion that this school is giving its pupils an acceptable standard of education, but it is a school with serious weaknesses. The reasons for this opinion are:
or
I am of the opinion that this school is underachieving. The reasons for this opinion are:

1

2

3

4

(Please continue on separate sheet if necessary.)

I confirm that I will report in these terms to the senior management team of the school and to the governors.

Signed ....

Name (please print) .... Date ..../.........../.........

Telephone number ....

Address ....

ANNEX 3

COMPLETING THE RECORD OF INSPECTION EVIDENCE

(A) COMPLETING THE *PRE-INSPECTION COMMENTARY*

What to include

The essential features of the *Pre-Inspection Commentary* are:

■ your preliminary views of the school in all areas of the *Evaluation Schedule;*

■ initial hypotheses, to be tested during the inspection, in each of these areas.

Using the *Pre-Inspection Commentary*

The evidence on which you base your views and hypotheses will come mainly from three sources, and you might find it helpful to structure your *Pre-Inspection Commentary* using these three areas. They are:

■ factual information from *Forms S1* and *S2;*

■ the school's previous inspection report;

■ qualitative information you gain from *Forms S3* and *S4* and your visit to the school.

You should complete the *Pre-Inspection Commentary* in two stages. You will be able to begin writing the commentary when you have received the previous report and the completed inspection forms, *Forms S1* and *S2*. The headteacher's responses on *Forms S3* and *S4* will give you a picture of the school's own view of itself. You will then have sufficient knowledge of the school to put together a set of questions to ask the headteacher on the preliminary visit.

The information you obtain from the preliminary visit will enable you to complete the *Pre-Inspection Commentary* so that all team members have a clear picture of the school, in all areas of the *Evaluation Schedule*, before the inspection begins.

At the end of each section of the commentary you should include one or two key hypotheses for the inspection team to test out. Try to avoid long lists of hypotheses and focus on the 'big issues'. There is no need to include the reporting requirements or the criteria from the *Evaluation Schedule* because you will use these as a matter of course to evaluate the evidence in all inspections. What is needed is a small number of issues, which are drawn clearly from the evidence so far available and which relate specifically to the school being inspected.

In most cases these hypotheses will need to be followed up by all inspectors, and in a SHORT INSPECTION this will certainly be the case. In a FULL INSPECTION, individual team members may need to focus on particular issues and report back to the team at a suitable team meeting. You may find it helpful to indicate in the *Pre-Inspection Commentary* how an issue will be followed up, and by whom.

Style of writing

The *Pre-Inspection Commentary* needs to be concise and to the point. You will most likely write in continuous prose in short paragraphs. You should not rehearse all the evidence you have considered, which is contained in the inspection forms and the school's documentation. Your commentary should contain your views, so far, of what you have seen and discussed. The hypotheses should also be brief and to the point.

Extract from* Pre-Inspection Commentary *partially completed before the preliminary visit to the school

Example before the school visit

2 How high are standards?	Interpretation of the school's results

Pre-inspection analysis of attainment:

Evaluation drawing on performance data, indicating Key Stages or groups of pupils, where relevant

Previous report:

- *Pupils' achievements were good or very good in 50 per cent of lessons and sound in the remainder*
- *English generally sound, good features in KS4*
- *Mathematics – satisfactory at pre-KS1 and good at KS4 but varied considerably in post-16; KS2 – good Y5 and Y6 but unsatisfactory in Y3 and Y4*
- *Science – satisfactory or better across all KS*
- *Music and PE – very good standards*
- *History, geography, DT – good standards, and satisfactory in the rest of the curriculum*

Satisfactory progress made in key skills of listening and speaking which pupils used well in all areas of the curriculum. Reading was well developed in most subjects; similarly the use of IT, even though some opportunities missed. The quality of learning was good in the majority of lessons. In most lessons pupils made good progress towards achieving their targets set in IEPs. Very little comment about the progress of pupils with PMLD and only passing reference to the sensory curriculum.

School documentation:

Nature of pupils' learning needs (SLD and PMLD) makes it inappropriate to compare their attainment to national norms. Recent test results were:
KS1 – All pupils working towards Level W
KS2 – In En and Ma, all pupils at Level W. In Sc, 2 pupils at Levels 1 or 2 in some elements
KS3 – All pupils at Level W in most subjects, although 3 pupils were assessed at Level 1 in Ma and SC
KS4 – No information available

- *Last year, 50 per cent of leavers went on to FE, the remainder to other routes*
- *Parents very satisfied with their children's progress and improvements in pupils' behaviour*
- *Well-documented procedures for attendance, behaviour, care and pastoral support – integration, where possible, is a central consideration*
- *Assessment and monitoring procedures are detailed and look a model of good practice*

Extract from the same **Pre-Inspection Commentary,** *showing the section written after the preliminary visit, and including the main issues for exploration during the inspection*

2   How high are standards?   Interpretation of the school's results

Pre-inspection analysis of attainment:

Evaluation drawing on performance data, indicating Key Stages or groups of pupils, where relevant

Pre-inspection visit:

The school's procedures for assessment and recording pupils' progress towards their personal and subject targets look very effective. Arrangements made to have full access to an agreed representative sample of pupils' files and records, including RoA – see separate detailed note on times and venues to meet pupils and staff concerned.

Developments in the curriculum and teaching, especially with PMLD pupils, look impressive – greater attention given to improving access and equal opportunities and to extending the scope and range of curriculum activities. The link with higher standards and faster rates of progress will need to be teased out. Evidence from being in classrooms, and talking with pupils and staff informally seems to be coherent with the main thrust of thinking behind much of the school's documentation and the general environment – it is a well-documented, lively and innovative school!

The key question is how all this impacts on pupils' achievements across the full curriculum and for particular groups of pupils and students.

Areas for further exploration:

1. *How effective are procedures for using information about pupils' progress towards their personal targets in their IEPs as the basis for whole school target-setting? Much is made of this in the documentation and the school believes it is setting challenging targets.*

2. *The school claims that pupils are making faster progress across the whole curriculum than was the case at the time of the previous inspection. What is the evidence for children under 5, for pupils with PMLD, for KS3 pupils and post-16 students? In addition, given the time and priority attached to SMSC and PSHE, are pupils and students benefiting in terms of better achievements in subjects and in personal development? Are standards even across all subjects, and is sufficient attention being given to communication, especially numeracy in KS4 and post-16?*

3. *The school has put much effort into supporting pupils with challenging behaviour and the evidence suggests that the pupils have been successful. What features of the school's practice have made the difference for the parents and youngsters involved?*

(B) COMPLETING THE *EVIDENCE FORM*

What to include

The *Evidence Form* is structured so that the same form can be used to record inspection evidence in four areas:

■ **lesson observations** (coded **L**), including the observation of small groups or individual tuition;

■ **analysis of pupils' work** (coded **A**), which might be undertaken independently of the pupils, or with the pupils present, to gain further insights into standards;

■ **discussions** (coded **D**) with pupils, staff, governors and others;

■ **any other evidence** (coded **O**), including observations of assemblies, registration periods, breaktimes, lunchtimes, arrival and departure from school and extra-curricular activities, and commentary on the school's documentation.

In writing each *Evidence Form*, you will need to complete the following parts:

■ the **context** in which the form has been completed;

■ the **evidence** you wish to record;

■ when used for lesson observations, and optionally in other cases, **grades** for: teaching; learning; attainment; and attitudes and values;

■ the **coding** boxes at the top.

Using the *Evidence Form*

Evidence Forms (EFs) are the key records of firsthand inspection evidence and your judgements on the basis of that evidence. You will need to refer to them when you identify strengths and weaknesses in your *Inspection Notebook*. They are also the source of illustrations for the inspection report.

When OFSTED's Inspection Quality Division monitors an inspection, the monitoring HMI may wish to look at the quality of evidence, judgement and grades recorded on *Evidence Forms*.

The context box

In the **context box**, put enough to describe the situation being recorded. If you are using the *EF* to record a discussion, say whom it is with and what it is about. If the *EF* is for a lesson or other observation, briefly describe what the teacher and pupils are doing so that someone else could visualise the situation you observed. If you are recording your analysis of pupils' work, include sufficient detail to identify the work with the relevant subject or subjects and year or Key Stage.

Example of a context box for a lesson observation

Context:

10 am. Lesson moving from mathematics to English and art. Two pupils leave for independence training using public transport. Pupils cutting and sticking to create death mask (topic work with CLA), using colour and shape creatively. T focuses upon reading with individuals.

Year 8/9 pupils with SLD

The evidence box

In the **evidence box** you should record the evidence you have collected and your judgements on the basis of that evidence. Each *EF* should contain:

- sufficient **evidence** to support the judgement(s) you make, in that anyone reading the evidence would be very likely to come to the same judgement;

Example of a lesson observation – recording evidence

Evidence:

Recognise and can sound letter 'v', also pupils building up their vocabulary of 'v' words evident in sounding names to pictures and filling in missing first letter to words. In discussion work, recount fully their activities in science, linked to months of year and birthdays, recounting a good deal of information confidently.

In response to story read, pupils show good levels of attention and comprehension. Able to relate story to pictures with confidence and much pleasure. Pick up cause-and-effect relationships, give good accounts of how people might feel about events and what are appropriate responses to different behaviour suggested by T.

Year 5–7 pupils with SLD – English lesson　　　　　**Learning – Grade 3; Attainment – Grade 7**

- a strong **focus on strengths and weaknesses**, and what makes them strengths and weaknesses, with less emphasis on that which is satisfactory but has no major positive or negative features;

Example of a lesson observation – recording strengths and weaknesses

Evidence:

T very skilled in managing lively pupils, sets and builds on challenging expectations by maintaining a brisk pace to learning. Reinforces learning skilfully, and offers praise and encouragement in equal measure.

Promotes pupils' positive self-image and affirmed personal integrity of individuals (to be confident and be responsible) within a carefully structured approach to learning objectives. T always gives good feedback and listens very carefully to what pupils say.

T makes skilled use of very good quality resources. Clear link in planning of learning objectives and T's knowledge of pupils' learning needs, IEP targets and routine assessment/recording procedures.

Two CLA are very alert to needs of potentially difficult pupils to whom they relate very well. Good joint-planning with T. Very effective individual support through use of tape recorders, signed sentences and pictures related to the story read by T.

Year 6/7 pupils with SLD – English lesson　　　　　**Learning and teaching – each Grade 2**

■ **illustrations** which can be drawn on by you or other inspectors when writing text for the report, particularly of strengths and weaknesses;

Example of a lesson observation – recording illustrations

Evidence:

Having been told the story of <u>Hamlet</u> and seen a video of the plot, the pupils have a good background knowledge to begin as a group to discuss the play and the characters. The dilemmas each of the characters faced discussed – the tragic figure of Ophelia and whether Hamlet was mad fully engages the pupils. They move on without fuss to write a short description of a character chosen by them, aided by a structured worksheet.

The lesson works well because of the excellent relationship between T, SSA and the pupils. The firm lesson structure creates space, opportunities and sufficient time to move towards mutually agreed goals. Together with the positive feedback the T enables all the pupils to contribute and encourage them to value each other's ideas. They all participate fully and with confidence in the group discussion.

Y9 pupils with EBD – English lesson   **Attitudes and behaviour – Grade 2; Teaching – Grade 2**

■ **judgements** made on the basis of the evidence and, in the case of lesson observations, summary judgements on teaching and learning, attainment, attitudes and behaviour;

Example of a lesson observation – recording judgements

Evidence:

Lesson objectives are clear and matched closely to pupils' needs. The music carefully chosen to encourage pupils to play the instruments fast and accurately. Initial hand-clapping sequence captured pupils' interest and helped them to concentrate as well as listen to themselves and others. Pupils were put into groups and this enabled T to give exercises within their capability. Pairing pupils works well – much good work in terms of co-operation.

Y3 pupils with MLD – music lesson   **Teaching – Grade 3**

■ **explanations** that justify why things are as they are.

Example of a lesson observation – recording explanations

Evidence:

Pupils gained much from this session because they know what they expected to learn and are familiar with the story's format. They are very keen to make suggestions about missing words and ideas to fit in with the story's plot. Above all they listen carefully to each other and are confident to try, even if they make mistakes. T's role is crucial in the quality of feedback given and way she spots children getting frustrated – SSAs alert too and offer reassuring words and eye-contact.

Y6 pupils with EBD – literacy lesson   **Learning – Grade 3**

You may wish additionally to use part of this space to record, for example the way pupils with English as an additional language are supported by the use of information and communications technology (ICT) in all subjects. This focused approach is most effective when used consistently by all members of the inspection team in every lesson observation.

The grade boxes

When you enter **grades** at the foot of the form, make sure they match the judgements in the text above about teaching and learning, attainment, and pupils' attitudes and behaviour. You should always grade lesson observations. You may find it helpful to grade *EF*s that record your analysis of pupils' work, and any *EF*s coded 0 in which there is an element of teaching, such as in an assembly or in some extra-curricular activities.

In **lesson observations** you must always grade **teaching, learning**, and pupils' **attitudes and behaviour**. In most cases you will use Grades 1–7 but you may need to use 0 if there is too little evidence to make a secure judgement. On very rare occasions, you may need to use 8 to indicate that it is not appropriate to enter a grade. Wherever possible, you should enter a grade for attainment. If you feel you do not have the expertise to make a judgement about attainment, for example if you are a lay inspector, it is acceptable to leave the attainment grade blank.

You should try to use the full range of grades. So, for example, if pupils' learning in a lesson is exemplary and you cannot see how it could be improved, award a Grade 1 and make sure that the text on the *EF* supports this grade.

Filling in the coded boxes at the top of the form

Every time you write an *EF* you need to code, where possible, the sections at the top of the form. The diagram shows what is needed. Further details are provided on the CD-ROM accompanying this *Handbook*.

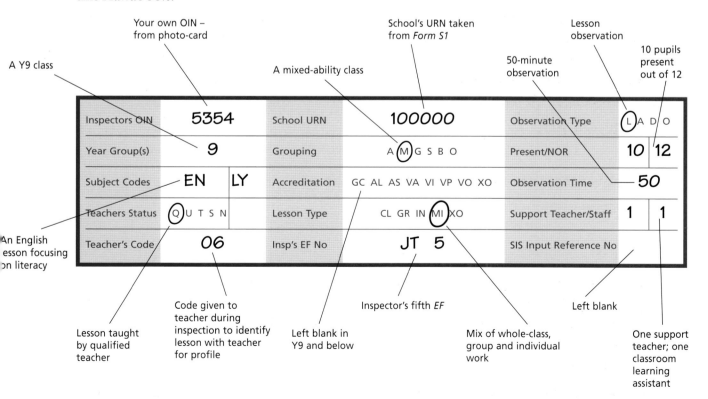

Style of writing

There is no prescribed format for completion of *EF*s. Effective writing could be in continuous prose or in note form; it could list strengths and weaknesses separately or cover the same ground within a single piece of text. What matters is that the *EF* communicates to others the essential features of what has been seen or discussed.

In **lesson observations**, the pieces of evidence you obtain for teaching and learning are often inextricably linked. When you write the *EF*, you should integrate these two areas whenever you can. You may wish to note particular points in each area that help you reach the two separate grades needed. If the grades for teaching and learning are different, for example if the teacher did all he or she could but other factors meant that pupils' learning was not graded as highly, you need to explain why they are different.

In the **analysis of pupils' records** you should primarily use the *EF* to give a clear picture of pupils' progress. Where this is relevant, you can use the *EF* to record the attainment of different groups of pupils and your exploration of differences in the standards achieved by pupils of different gender or ethnic background. You should also try, where you can, to bring out any evidence about teaching, pupils' learning and personal development.

> ### *Example of recording the analysis of pupils work*
>
> **Context:**
>
> *Extract from an analysis of post-16 students' work*
>
> **Evidence:**
>
> *Records indicate that students are making good progress in personally set targets in home skills, such as cooking and washing, and in travel skills. For example, it is now evident that five students can now cook simple meals without help – something they could not do six months ago.*

When you write about **discussions** with pupils, staff, governors/key members of the appropriate authority or others, you should record the key points of the discussion, not try to transcribe all of what was said. This is often easier if the discussion takes place using a set of headings designed specifically for that occasion. At the end of the discussions, if there is time, you might find it helpful to go briefly through what you have written to check you have the main points accurately recorded.

Example of record of a discussion with ICT co-ordinators

Context:

Extract from a record of a discussion with the ICT co-ordinator about leadership and management role of co-ordinator

Evidence:

HT and governors had responded to the concerns expressed about weaknesses in provision highlighted in the previous inspection but not acted upon until the appointment of the present co-ordinator. No satisfactory explanation given for the delayed action – to follow up in discussion with HT.

Involved staff in discussions about needs, and used skills audit of all staff (not just teachers) to identify existing levels of expertise and interest as well as training needs. Staff very responsive and eager to tackle their own INSET needs – some felt they needed help as parents to understand what their own children could do on computers!

The recent expenditure on equipment replacement and programmes purchased has been examined by the governors' finance sub-committee. For the first time, the governors have used a simple model for testing cost-effectiveness. Co-ordinator has clearly been influential in working with linked governor.

Evidence from lesson observation points clearly to good use made of IT, growing staff confidence and pupils being supported to achieve higher standards. Gains in their self-confidence are very noticeable, especially in KS4 and post-16.

(C) COMPLETION OF *INSPECTION NOTEBOOKS*

What to include

On FULL INSPECTIONS and on SHORT INSPECTIONS, where it is used, the *Inspection Notebook* should always include:

- judgements in as many areas of the *Evaluation Schedule* as possible for which you have evidence, expressed as strengths and weaknesses;

- references to the *Evidence Forms* which form the basis for these judgements, and which can be used to illustrate them, if needed, in the inspection report;

- an overall evaluation under each *Evaluation Schedule* heading for which you have evidence.

When you are inspecting a subject or more than one subject during a FULL INSPECTION, your *Notebook* should additionally contain:

- a section on pre-inspection evidence about those subjects, written using the guidance given above for completing the *Pre-Inspection Commentary*;

- a summary of the feedback you intend to give to the co-ordinator for each subject you are inspecting, at or towards the end of the inspection;

- grades for the judgement recording statements in each of the subjects you are responsible for;

- the time you have spent on firsthand inspection in the school.

In a FULL INSPECTION, when you are responsible for writing aspects or subject sections of the report, the *Inspection Notebook* will also contain:

■ the draft text of your contributions to the inspection report, usually completed after the final team meeting.

Using the *Inspection Notebook*

Each inspector, including the registered inspector, must complete an *Inspection Notebook* in a FULL INSPECTION, and the completed form will be entered into the inspection software. You may use one in a SHORT INSPECTION if you find it convenient to do so, but its contents will not be entered into the inspection software. It will, however, form part of the evidence base for the inspection.

The *Inspection Notebook* is for you to record your own views and judgements on the evidence you have collected. You should use it after you have reflected on the evidence from a number of sources. For example, after seeing several lessons on the first day of an inspection, you will probably feel you have sufficient evidence about teaching to record your views and make some tentative judgements about the quality of teaching. You should express your views as strengths and weaknesses. There is no need to include extensive commentary on things that are satisfactory. These views would form the basis of your contribution to the inspection team's discussions about teaching at a team meeting. You would be able to illustrate your points by referring back to the evidence on your *Evidence Forms*. For this reason, you will need to include a reference to the source(s) of evidence against each judgement recorded.

You will probably find that, in some areas of the *Evaluation Schedule*, you will be combining evidence from a range of different sources before writing in your *Inspection Notebook*. For example, your views on pupils' behaviour will come from *Evidence Forms* covering lessons, what you have seen outside lessons and discussions with staff and pupils.

In FULL INSPECTIONS, where you are inspecting more than one subject or aspect, you will need to structure your *Notebook* according to the subjects and/or aspects you are responsible for. If you are responsible for inspecting more than one subject, you will need to complete a judgement recording form for each. Your *Notebook* should incorporate the evidence from other team members who may have inspected work in 'your' subjects.

Whether you fill in your *Inspection Notebook* by hand or using a computer, you should treat it as a running commentary, which can be modified and added to as the inspection proceeds.

Towards the end of the inspection, you will need to make an overall evaluation of the evidence you have obtained under each heading in the *Evaluation Schedule*. You will also need to make sure that all the strengths and weaknesses recorded represent your final considered judgements, as these will be entered into the inspection software with the other inspection information.

You will also need to record the source(s) from which you derived each judgement. This will be a reference to one or more *Evidence Forms*, possibly from other inspectors on the team. In a FULL INSPECTION you will need copies of these forms if you are writing a subject or aspect, so that you can refer to them after the inspection has finished.

When an inspection is monitored by OFSTED's Inspection Quality Division, the monitoring HMI may wish to look at the quality of evaluations and judgements contained in *Inspection Notebooks*.

The subject judgement recording form

Towards or at the end of each FULL INSPECTION, you will need to enter grades in each subject inspected for the judgement recording statements at the back of the *Inspection Notebook*. The numbering follows that of the school judgement recording statements in the *Record of Corporate Judgements*. The grades should fall naturally into place from the judgements you have recorded in the earlier pages of the *Inspection Notebook*. If assigning a grade is difficult, it probably indicates that you have not already made or not recorded a clear judgement. In these circumstances you are advised to go back to consider the judgement itself, making use of the strengths and weaknesses you have recorded and, if necessary, referring to *Evidence Forms*.

Style of writing

You use the *Inspection Notebook* to record judgements, summarise your views and point to the evidence on which they are based. It should be written very concisely, therefore. It should consist of:

- single-sentence statements, or the equivalent in note form;

- coded references to *Evidence Forms*, using the code entered in the box at the top of each relevant form.

3   How well are pupils or students taught?   Teaching and learning

What is the quality of teaching and what is its impact?

Strengths and weaknesses from the inspection, indicating groups of pupils and Key Stages where relevant, and an overall evaluation.

	Sources of evidence:

Strengths:

- *Planning of lessons generally satisfactory and preparation of work is thorough. SSAs generally deployed well – at best they make a significant impact upon the quality of provision*   —   *EF21, 41*

- *Good relationships in all lessons – teachers and adults good at encouraging positive attitudes and co-operation between pupils*   —   *EF41, 42*

- *Assessment very good – use of 'post-it' system is very sophisticated and effective*   —   *EF13, 15, 17*

- *Post-16 students given considerable responsibility*   —   *EF3, 9, 17*

Weaknesses:

- *Some poor time management, pupils insufficiently stimulated*   —   *EF16, 18*

- *Unclear about learning objectives, confused with teaching activities in some classes*   —   *EF21, 22*

- *Fragmented series of expectations and some age-inappropriate activities and resources*   —   *EF39*

Summary view on teaching:

- *Good in post-16*

- *Common approaches in most classes for planning, assessment, record-keeping which were positive features*

- *Relationships and social development*

- *Confusion of activities/targets with 'outcomes', leads to a lack of focus and clarity to much of the work in a couple of classes*

(D) COMPLETION OF THE *RECORD OF CORPORATE JUDGEMENTS*

What to include

The *Record of Corporate Judgements* for your inspection must include:

- corporate judgements of the inspection team in each area of the *Evaluation Schedule*;

- agreed grades for each of the judgement recording statements required in your inspection;

- agreed grades for each of the additional judgement recording statements *P1–P10*;

- agreed grades and, where necessary, reasons for changes of grade, to the similar school comparisons;

- statements and, where necessary, reasons for your decisions about whether the school requires special measures, has serious weaknesses or is underachieving;

- a summary of the extent and range of the inspection evidence.

Using the *Record of Corporate Judgements*

A single *Record of Corporate Judgements (RCJ)* is used in each inspection. It is completed at team meetings towards the end of an inspection and/or at the final team meeting after the inspection. You should use the *Record of Corporate Judgements* to record the team's agreed judgements and point to the evidence on which they are based. When parts of the *RCJ* are completed at an earlier team meeting, the contents of these parts will need to be confirmed at the final team meeting after the inspection. Because, as the registered inspector, you will be managing these meetings, it will be helpful if the actual recording is carried out by another member of the team, leaving you free to focus on the team's judgements.

The order of the pages in the *Record of Corporate Judgements* is designed to support the final inspection team meeting by moving from the detail of what was known before the inspection, through the evidence base collected during the inspection, to the evaluation of the effectiveness of the school. In short, you are expected to use the *Record of Corporate Judgements* to bring all your judgements together and reach some overall conclusions.

The main strengths and weaknesses are expressed, in draft form, as they will appear in the relevant boxes in the summary of the inspection report, namely WHAT THE SCHOOL DOES WELL and WHAT COULD BE IMPROVED. The *Record of Corporate Judgements* also gives space to draft the matters that the 'appropriate authority' must include in its post-inspection action plan. These should match exactly the entries in the section WHAT COULD BE IMPROVED.

The final team meeting represents the culmination of the collection of evidence, testing out hypotheses and reaching tentative judgements, which are then confirmed, or otherwise. The *Record of Corporate Judgements* is a way of ensuring that the team's agreed judgements are recorded so that they can be used as the basis for writing the inspection report. Individual inspectors will be able to contribute a range of strengths or weaknesses in each section of the *Evaluation Schedule* and the team needs to weigh these up, making reference to the evidence base where necessary, to reach corporate judgements. Once these judgements have been agreed, it is a relatively easy task for the team to assign grades to the judgement recording statements.

You will also need to record the source from which the judgement stems. This might be a reference to an *Inspection Notebook* or it might be a reference to one or more *Evidence Forms*. If you refer to an *Inspection Notebook*, you will need to ensure that it contains the reference to the *Evidence Forms*.

You should use the *Record of Corporate Judgements* carefully and record only the significant points you wish to include in the inspection report. You should record all the required judgements you will need for the summary report, so that when you come to write it, all the necessary information will be to hand. When you, and in some cases others, come to write the commentary section of the report, you will need to expand these points, drawing on explanatory and illustrative material from *Inspection Notebooks* and *Evidence Forms*.

The school judgement recording form

You will need to end your discussions of each section of the *Evaluation Schedule* by grading the judgement recording statements relevant to your inspection. In SHORT INSPECTIONS, the statements will be those at the top of the list of statements, printed in bold typeface. In FULL INSPECTIONS, you will also need to grade the more detailed statements printed in italic typeface.

If assigning a grade is difficult, it probably indicates that a clear corporate judgement has not been reached and you are advised to go back to consider the judgement itself, making use of the strengths, weaknesses and illustrations contributed by members of the inspection team. Having reconsidered the judgement, and possibly having re-written it in the *Record of Corporate Judgements*, the grade should fall naturally into place.

The ten judgement recording statements in the *Record of Corporate Judgements* not connected directly with an *Evaluation Schedule* heading (P1–P10) are pointers to what the report contains, not judgements in themselves. For example, *Statement P1* is not about whether the attainment of boys and girls is different, but about whether the report contains such a judgement. You can, therefore, usually answer these straightforwardly with *Yes* or *No*.

Guidance on reaching conclusions about whether the school requires special measures, has serious weaknesses, or is underachieving, is given in Annex 2.

The summary of the extent of inspection evidence at the end of the *Record of Corporate Judgements* is completed by collating the times and evidence bases from each *Inspection Notebook* used. In SHORT INSPECTIONS, you will need to ask the other members of the inspection team to inform you of their contribution as it will not always be recorded in an *Inspection Notebook*.

Style of writing

Because the *Record of Corporate Judgements* is a summary of the team's inspection judgements, it should be written very concisely. It should consist of:

- single-sentence statements, or the equivalent in note form;

- coded references to *Inspection Notebooks* and *Evidence Forms*, using the entries in the bottom centre box at the top of each relevant *Evidence Form*.

7   How well is the school led and managed?

How effectively do the leadership and management of the school contribute to pupils' achievements?

Main strengths and weaknesses, indicating groups of pupils and Key Stages where relevant, sources of evidence, and an overall evaluation.

Sources of evidence:

Strengths:

- Day-to-day management of the school effective — EF33

- School runs smoothly and functions as an orderly community with a very positive ethos — EF22, 24, 25

- Time-keeping and punctuality are generally satisfactory — EF32, 61

- Organisation and management of pupils' records are good — EF4

- Some (but not all) strategies for monitoring work are effective — EF18, 20, 27, 28

- Financial planning is good; staff and resources carefully deployed – value for money satisfactory — EF59

Weaknesses:

- Medium and long-term strategic planning have unsatisfactory features due mainly to lack of clarity and direction from HT and governors; best value principles applied inconsistently — EF23, 52, 59

- In some key areas (KS4) there is an evident lack of rigour in monitoring of teaching — EF53

- Curriculum co-ordinators have a very difficult task in covering the 3–19 age range and there is no consistent evidence of them having a significant impact on the quality of work — EF40, 47, 51, 54, 60

- The quality of policy documentation in subjects does not match that for more general school issues — PIC

Overall evaluation:

- Effective and efficient at day-to-day level

- Medium and long-term strategic planning and development are unsatisfactory

ANNEX 4

NATIONAL EDUCATIONAL INITIATIVES

Increasingly, inspections will take place in schools that are involved in a network, project or scheme which receives specific funding to promote particular educational goals such as raising standards.

The inspection report must refer to such involvement in the INFORMATION ABOUT THE SCHOOL section. You should also report on any impact on quality and standards in the school, which accrues from involvement in the project.

In some inspections, much more detailed evaluation of the project and its impact will feature through section 9 of the *Evaluation Schedule*. In such cases, additional time will be added to the inspection contract, and OFSTED will provide supplementary guidance on the inspection of the issue concerned.

This annex sets out background information about three initiatives in which some special schools and pupil referral units may be involved.

1. EARLY EXCELLENCE CENTRES

Purpose

Early Excellence Centres (EECs) aim to be models for the development of integrated early years services. They aim to bring together high-quality early learning, childcare and family support services for those children and parents who need them. They should be catalysts for the development of good practice in the areas and regions they serve, and for spreading new ideas and providing innovative services.

Key features

Early Excellence Centres usually incorporate one or more nursery schools or classes. They will:

- be multidisciplinary, by drawing together education, care, adult education, private and voluntary providers and employers to collaborate in providing one-stop services;

- have a strong emphasis on staff training and development, and outreach support for parents and other providers;

- include support for parents who need help with parenting skills and literacy, for example enabling parents to attend classes in the same centre as their children;

- allow parents who work or are training for work to have access to integrated education and childcare for their children;

- ensure that parents of children with special educational needs can look forward to early assessment of their child's needs and a planned programme of linked provision, including support for the parents themselves, where appropriate.

Inspection focus

You should evaluate only the direct impact of the activities of the EEC on the educational aspects of the school you are inspecting, as set out in the *Evaluation Schedule*. Features may include the enhanced involvement of parents, students or others in the education provided. You must not evaluate the work or impact of other professional services, such as medical, social or psychological services, in relation to the school.

2. EDUCATION ACTION ZONES

Purpose

Education Action Zones (EAZs) are a key part of government policy to raise standards in areas which face challenging circumstances in terms of underachievement or disadvantage. They receive extra funding from government, business and industry. A partnership forum, which sets out an action plan to raise standards, runs them. They are freed from some statutory requirements.

Key features

Education Action Zones:

- are established in less favoured parts of the country;
- invite an innovative contribution from business;
- have government funding of at least £250,000 per annum matched by business funding;
- address local problems;
- focus on teaching and learning;
- may suspend the National Curriculum;
- could change teachers' pay and conditions;
- may employ Advanced Skills Teachers;
- are organised in different ways.

Centrally, they exist to raise educational achievement in the areas they serve.

Inspection focus

Evaluate how particular EAZ initiatives contribute to the effectiveness of the leadership and management of the school. For example, there may be:

- mentors from business working with headteachers;
- business expertise to improve teachers' skills at middle-management level;
- business help in target-setting.

You must evaluate the contribution of an EAZ against your assessment of its prime purpose, the likelihood or actuality of the EAZ raising standards achieved.

3. EXCELLENCE IN CITIES

Purpose

Excellence in Cities provides a new framework for inner-city schools. The initiative aims to raise standards and aspirations in bigger cities. It is designed to ensure that every gifted pupil is stretched and that a full range of special needs is met. The aim of the programme is to extend diversity and excellence by tackling low expectations and any other barriers to learning.

Key features

The initiative includes:

- a radical approach to the needs of gifted and talented children;
- an encouragement to schools to use setting to meet individual aptitudes and abilities;
- developing new tests to stretch the most able;
- tackling disruption in schools through learning support units;
- providing the support of learning mentors to every pupil who needs one;
- establishing new university summer schools for 16–17-year-olds in the inner-city.

Inspection focus

Like EAZs, the purpose of the initiative is to raise standards. If you are inspecting a school which is part of the Excellence in Cities initiative, your evaluation should give a clear view of the initiative's effect on the standards achieved and on any other factors which have an impact on standards, such as teaching and leadership and management. You should be able to identify positive benefits from the initiative across all aspects of the school. In particular, this should be evident in the standards achieved by gifted and talented pupils.

INDEX

Printed in the United Kingdom for The Stationery Office   J0091743   C100   12/99